Other Books by Seon Manley
PUBLISHED BY THE VANGUARD PRESS

RUDYARD KIPLING:
Creative Adventurer

NATHANIEL HAWTHORNE:
Captain of the Imagination

ADVENTURES IN MAKING:
The Romance of Crafts Around the World

JAMES JOYCE:
Two Decades of Criticism

Dorothy and William

WORDSWORTH

COTTAGES IN THE LAKE COUNTRY

Illustration by Joseph Pennell

Dorothy and William
WORDSWORTH:
The Heart of a Circle
of Friends

BY SEON MANLEY

THE VANGUARD PRESS INC.
NEW YORK

This book is for my godson,

Benjamin Moore Belcher III, "Jamie,"

with my love.

❧ Contents ☙

Contents

❧ *Illustrations* ❧

Dorothy and William

WORDSWORTH

❧ *I* ❦

There was a boy . . .
and a girl

Pull the primrose, sister Anne!
Pull as many as you can.
—Here are daisies, take your fill;
Pansies, and the cuckoo-flower:
Of the lofty daffodil
Make your bed, or make your bower;
Fill your lap, and fill your bosom;
Only spare the strawberry-blossom!

from: Foresight
by: William Wordsworth

It had been a perfect spring. As the boy, William, walked along the road, it seemed to him that primroses sprang up as he passed; violets that had not been there yesterday appeared today. Strawberries were struggling to come to fruition and the pilwort, a wildflower, was, as his sister said, "like gold in the sun."

The boy watched his sister move along the bank of the river. They seemed to be parts of one another: the river, the boy, and the girl.

Most boys resented their sisters, but William, as he watched Dorothy move with the ease and sudden joy of the flowing stream, found her laughter as pleasing and comforting as the cry of the birds. She noticed everything. Sometimes she would point to the snow, in patches at the top of the mountain, or she would break off a twig from a birch tree, or call William to come and stroke some bright green ivy. Being younger, she would often take off her cumbersome stockings and wade in the icy water.

This was William's favorite river in all the world. True, he had not seen much of the world, but he had seen the sea and many lakes, and of all of the waters, this river, the Derwent, was the finest.

He loved the shire of Cumberland where he had been born.

Many thought it the most beautiful of all the English land-scapes. But it was not only its beauty that appealed to William; it was its proud past. Cockermouth Castle dominated history even as it did the scene for William and his sister. Now the castle was decayed and partially in ruins, yet the boy, calling upon imagination to re-create the past, could still see the flag tower and the great gatehouse and the names and coats of arms of famous families. The still-standing walls seemed like great bows of ships, and if you climbed to the top of the castle, you could look down at the Derwent River below. Years later, when William became England's most fa-mous poet, he described his river as "a voice that flowed along my dreams."

When Dorothy and William were very young, their world had been bounded by their garden and their river. But be-yond had been a road that fascinated William, who felt him-self a wanderer, an explorer. Later he was to say that he had accepted "an invitation into space." He was eager to explore the new world opening up all around him, and to guide other people to it. His excitement and sense of adventure often made him think he was a mariner, sailing the roaring sea, or one of the vagabonds who constantly roamed the hills of his birthplace.

At one time you might run across an old pedlar, at another a beggar woman or a man gathering leeches. As William looked at them, he knew they all had their own stories. Tales did not belong to kings and queens alone; simple people, too, could have stories. Of course, there were royal stories about his own village. Almost a Border town, it had all the excitement and superstition of the Border area, which was transfixed between practical England and romantic Scot-land. It was to Cockermouth Castle that Mary, Queen of

Scots, had come with sixteen followers after she had been badly defeated in her attempt to gain control of the British crown. It was here that the wealthy Henry Fletcher was said to have given her quantities of crimson velvet and dressed her as the queen she was, after taking away the soiled and dusty garments in which she had made her escape. Mary, Queen of Scots, had been free here; she was not to be so again. Her imprisonment was imminent and her death was not far away.

William always shuddered at the word "death." It had been in the appalling darkness of the tower of Cockermouth Castle that he had first imagined what death might be like. He had simply shrugged his shoulders at the thought and gone out into the sun. Leaving the tower, he would usually go to the river because its sound soothed him as much as the remembered sound of his mother's voice.

The Lake District, in the northwest of England, has always been one of the most beautiful and romantic regions in England and in English poetry. The area circles, for roughly ninety miles, rivers, lakes, valleys, and mountains, all carved and dug by ancient glaciers. It seems to be a part of the world particularly responsive to the change of season, being a deep green in summer, crimson and rust in the fall. It is a place of primroses, daffodils, bluebells—and poets. William Wordsworth, born in the village of Cockermouth on April 7, 1770, seemed to inherit the spirit and beauty of this country. Later, he would try to re-create its springlike glory in his poetry.

William's sister, Dorothy, was born more than twenty months later, in the same multi-windowed house in Cockermouth. Early childhood there, for both of them, was pleasant. William remembered later how he had tried to swim in the Derwent River when he was just five years old, and how he would sometimes run naked through his father's fields, where

4

the yellow weeds seemed almost like trees to him. His mother had given him and his sister one of the greatest of all gifts: the ability to respond deeply to nature.

Both of Wordsworth's parents—his mother, Ann Cookson, and his father, John Wordsworth—were from old families of the North of England. Their first boy, Richard, had, even as a small infant, a pragmatic approach to life. He was not to be an adventurer. Instead, he would become a lawyer. William, the child of spring, and Dorothy, born on Christmas Day, 1771, were far different. They had in them the deep cry of imagination and the soul of explorers. So, too, had their younger brother John. He was what William and Dorothy were to call "a silent poet." Particularly loved by William and Dorothy, he was always shy and lonely. His father called him Ibex because the ibex is the shyest of all beasts. Then came their brother Christopher, good with books, a scholar at heart.

John Wordsworth, the head of the family, was a hard-working lawyer, who covered the countryside as an agent for a great landowner, Sir James Lowther. At home, however, John Wordsworth would gather his children around him and recite by heart great chunks of Shakespeare, Milton, and Spenser. William and Dorothy, and later John, were excited by what William would later call "the Forests of Romance."

As children, William and Dorothy had loathed the "goody" stories, or instructive tales, that were recommended for young people at that time. Instead, they loved the old legends of the Border, the tales of Scottish chiefs, and the traditional folktales of the countryside. It was important to immerse oneself in stories and in poetry, Wordsworth thought. It was important to open a window into the imagination, and although some of the old tales and legends might be filled with fear, they had to be part of his childhood. Later, Wordsworth was to say

5

that the best reading for children was legend and tale. "Oh! give us once again the Wishing-Cap," he wrote. The invisible coat of Jack the Giant Killer, Robin Hood, and Sabra in the forest with St. George—a child who knew such legends was able to forget himself, said Wordsworth, and that was a precious gain. Even tales of terror fascinated William, and when he had grown to manhood he never forgot the horror of a hanged man's grave.

One day he had been especially filled with eagerness. Having just learned to ride, he felt the power of independence overtake him. He was about five years old, but to ride one's own horse showed that manhood was on the way. He liked the feel of the animal moving smoothly beneath him; he liked riding in the mist, the dampness circling his head and the horse's hoofs sloshing in the wet May ground, moist and soft after the hard winter. But he liked company, too, and so with him that day rode one of his most treasured companions, James, the groom from his grandfather's stable in Penrith.

The town of Penrith, the home of Wordsworth's grandparents, had been the capital of old Cumbria, which later became the shire of Cumberland. Constantly attacked by Scottish raiders coming across the Border, it was the home of the Jacobite rebels who favored the cause of Mary, Queen of Scots. It had, as Cockermouth did, a shattered castle, old and ivy-ridden, to which clung stories and adventures that delighted young William. For two centuries the castle had been used to guard the border and thus its great tower was called Border Tower, or Beacon Hill Tower. One could go up to its highest point to see if troops were massing on the other side of the border. All the Wordsworth children spent long periods at Penrith in their early years, and William, as a young boy, often imagined raiders pouring through the woodland, climbing over the crags, and pouring into the village itself.

Beacon Hill greatly attracted William, and on that May day he probably encouraged James to take him to the top of the tower to see the world that lay below. It was a trip he was to take often in later years—always with excitement and pleasure—but that day there was more than the usual excitement, and it was to haunt him and cause some strange "association" in his mind that was somehow to give him an image for poetry and a kind of "stopping of time." It made him aware of himself.

The trip had been joyous, as the pony went well, but somewhere William, exulting in his new independence, galloped ahead of the groom and became lost. At first the boy was delighted. He was alone and a horseman, holding the bridle as well as any man. He dismounted and started to lead his horse down the rough, stony moor. Stumbling, the horse and boy finally managed to make the descent, reaching a spot "Where in former times a murderer had been hung in iron chains."

The gibbet mast from which the murderer had been hanged was still standing at the very spot on which he had committed his murder. Most of the wood had decayed. On the turf close by, some villager had carved the murderer's name.

Young William stood terrified, yet entranced, his imagination opening to all the superstitions of the neighborhood. He had heard the story. He knew a murderer had been buried there but he had never expected to come upon his grave. He knew that each year grass covered over the murderer's name, and that each year someone would go to the spot, clear the grass away, and leave the letters "fresh and visible."

He stood, frightened, and then, moving as rapidly as he could, he climbed to the bare field again and saw, standing near the Beacon Tower, a girl—a simple village girl with a pitcher on her head. It was an ordinary sight, but it produced upon him some kind of visionary dream; one of those images that stood out; something that taught him about associations, a word that was to become important to the philosophy of the century in which he lived and the type of poetry that was developed from it.

Throughout his life he would be aware of these sudden, sharp images, sights that stayed in his mind so painfully he could not erase them unless he exorcised them in words. As a child, of course, he did not have the words, and he simply shook with terror and remembered.

Superstitions were particularly strong in the latter part of the eighteenth century, and the Wordsworth children seemed to run across more than their usual share of them. Even the old healing power of "the Queen's touch" was still remembered by people in Wordsworth's day. George III, King of England at the time William was five, did not believe in such power, but was disliked in any case. He was "no good at all," so his touch would not have helped. Earlier, Queen Anne had had the royal touch, and Samuel Johnson remembered that when he was ill as a boy he had been taken, at the doctor's suggestion, to be "touched" by Queen Anne. He had "a confused but somehow a sort of solemn recollection of a lady in diamonds and a long black hood."

If there was no "royal touch" during William and Dorothy's childhood, there were all sorts of other strange cures. For example, part of the gibbet mast where the murderer had been hanged supposedly contained magic. People would steal such relics and sell them. Children wore all sorts of charms around their necks: amber for the eyes, orris root for the neck, rings of nails if they were subject to fits. There were even advertisements for miracle necklaces. After wearing them for only one night, children "who but just before were on the brink of the grave with their teeth, fits, fevers, convulsions, grips, looseness . . ." would immediately cut their teeth with safety.

Remarkably, the Wordsworth family was emancipated from some of the more primitive ideas of the period, but nonetheless, as the children roamed around the countryside, they came in contact with many of the rural customs of the time. They waited expectantly each year for the New Year carolers who came singing:

> *Here we come a-wassailing*
> *Among the leaves so green,*
> *Here we come a-wassailing*
> *So fair to be seen.*

And then all the children would join in the chorus:

> *Love and joy come to you*
> *And to your wassail too,*
> *And God send you a happy New Year*
> *And God send you a happy New Year.*
> *Our wassail cup is made of the Rosemary Tree*
> *So is our beer of the best boralea.*

They knew of the old custom of Shrove Tuesday, when children went around begging for a piece of home-cured bacon, crying "Pray, dame, a collop." They knew the simple habit of the countryside on All Fools' Day, when you sent your friends on false errands for pigeon's milk or strap oil, or for something like a guttering peg that never existed. On Good Friday the mouth-watery chant of "Hot Cross buns, Hot Cross buns, Smoking hot, piping hot," rang in the spring air.

Despite the continuation of old customs, the young Wordsworths were growing up in a new, explosive period—an age of reason—in which an effort was being made to educate the child. Previously, it had been thought that "children should

9

be seen and not heard"; now there was some attempt to understand the child, to let him run free, to develop himself.

The Wordsworths were lucky to enjoy the freedom of the great outdoors. There were many children who were still miserably flogged and some who were treated roughly in order that they might be "hardened up." The poet Robert Southey, who was later to live with the Wordsworths in the Lake District, recalled that he had a little sister who had died of hydrocephalus. "The disease," he wrote, "may have been induced by their dipping her every morning in a tub of the coldest well water. This was done from an old notion of strengthening her; the shock was dreadful, the poor child's horror of it every morning when taken out of bed even more so. I cannot remember having seen it without horror, nor do I believe that among the preposterous practices which false theories have produced there was a more cruel or parless [*sic*] one than that." Some children wore an iron collar around their neck to strengthen their back. Dry bread and cold food was often their daily diet; all else was indulgence.

Even at the end of the eighteenth century, education for girls was considered almost unnecessary. If one could read and write, cast accounts, and do housekeeping and needlework, that was all one needed. To acquire knowledge was something else. "A woman's learning," says a periodical of the time, "is like the fine clothes of an upstart who is anxious to exhibit to all the world the riches so unexpectedly acquired." Some girls were fortunate. One who was to become a friend of Dorothy Wordsworth's and who had the same longing for learning, Mary Lamb, "tumbled early by accident or design, into a spacious closet of good old English reading without much selection or prohibition." William and Dorothy particularly enjoyed tumbling in that closet.

Nor were the young Wordsworths overly protected from

COCKERMOUTH CASTLE

Illustration by Joseph Pennell

the more pathetic sights of the countryside. As the eighteenth century closed, the country laborer grew poorer. A man might work for what amounted to a dollar a week. Families were large, and many children were sent out into the fields to work. Sometimes they might make only a penny a day working, but their job was better than that of the child in the city or town who was up at four in the morning to work all day in a factory.

All children went to work at an early age. Wordsworth's brother Richard was articled to a lawyer at fourteen, while his brother John went to sea at twelve.

The Industrial Revolution had dawned with thunder over the land and it was to affect England and Wordsworth, who was to become the country's greatest nineteenth-century poet, with the force of a violent storm.

Just as William remembered the murderer's grave, other scenes were to stay with him: a man in rags, but one with great individuality; a woman in tatters, but somehow radiant. Sometime in those very early days, the concept of the individual in conflict with society began to emerge in Wordsworth's mind.

It was to be an age of revolution. The British colony across the ocean had dumped tea into Boston Harbor, and a revolution was under way—a revolution for the individual —for democracy; a revolution to put aside forever such old customs as the royal Queen's touch. In France still another revolution was brewing, one that would have even closer meaning for young William. Both these revolutions sought to express new ideas, and new poets were needed to attempt to reconcile the thoughts of the old century and those of the new.

Born as he was near the last quarter of the eighteenth century, Wordsworth was to speak for both the old and the new, the nineteenth century. He was fortunate to find the words welling from a source deep within him; fortunate, too, in the time in which he lived, a time that also produced such writers as his sister, Dorothy Wordsworth, Mary and Charles Lamb, Jane Austen, and Samuel Taylor Coleridge; a time that produced such scientists as Sir Humphrey Davy, and such painters as Joseph Turner and John Constable.

Most fortunate of all, William had a constant source of inspiration, his sister Dorothy, about whom he said:

> *The Blessing of my later years*
> *Was with me when a boy:*
> *She gave me eyes, she gave me ears;*
> *And humble cares, and delicate fears;*
> *A heart, the fountain of sweet tears,*
> *And love, and thought, and joy.*

❧ II ❧

The Seekers

—A simple Child,
That lightly draws its breath,
And feels its life in every limb,
What should it know of death?

from: We Are Seven
by: William Wordsworth

Then, suddenly, those days of sunlight grew black for the very young Dorothy and her brothers. When William was just quite eight years old, his sister barely six, their mother died. The children, particularly Dorothy and William, were to draw together tightly when, as Wordsworth remembered later, they were left

> *destitute and as we might,*
> *Trooping together.*

They were not together long. At the time the children felt a need to stay bound most closely as a family unit, John Wordsworth, their father, was too tormented to keep them with him. Perhaps they reminded him of his dead wife; in any case, he was away far too much to leave the young children alone. He did what he thought best—he sent them away.

His mistake, perhaps, was sending them to different places. Years later, William, Dorothy, and particularly John, felt an extreme need to be together, as though they had to make up for all those years in which they were apart.

Dorothy, the most defenseless and one of the youngest, was moved from one relative to another: first to Aunt Elizabeth Threlkeld at Halifax; then to her Penrith grandparents, who seemed remarkably unsympathetic to the child; finally to Aunt and Uncle Cookson, whom she grew to love deeply.

We know very little of the early years of Dorothy's life, but we do know that, like her brother William, she responded, perhaps even over-responded, to the world around her. When she found words to express her feelings she knew a deep happiness. But sometimes, as when in childhood she first looked upon the ocean, tears were her only reaction.

Miss Threlkeld, in the gracious spirit of the age, opened her home not only to Dorothy but to the children of her dead sister, Mrs. Ferguson. Here Dorothy learned the give and take of being with other children. Nonetheless, she longed always for that best of all playmates—her brother William—whom she did not see again until his schooldays were almost over.

The world did not close down quite so much on William. When his brothers joined him at the Grammar School in Hawkshead they had a semblance of family life with the house mother of their cottage, Ann Tyson.

As a young boy, William Wordsworth had an impetuous nature. His mother had sensed this quality in him as a small child. He was destined, she said, for either good or evil.

William, too, began early to think of himself as being a little apart, a wanderer among men in a landscape that had about it "something rich and strange."

As he grew older he thought of his work as a journey into himself; he saw himself as a seeker. He expressed a new revolutionary psychology that recognized man as a complex being who had many contradictory emotions. Whether he admitted it or not, Wordsworth's theme was, as he called it, "What passed within me." He said that man had hiding places of great power. The psychologist William James later expressed this same idea. "We have," said James, "a dumb region of the heart in which we dwell alone." From this "dumb region of the heart" came communication and, as Wordsworth knew, creativity:

> *Of genius, power,*
> *Creation and divinity itself*
> *I have been speaking, for my theme has been*
> *What passed within me. Not of outward things,*
> *Done visibly for other minds, words, signs,*
> *Symbols or actions, but of my own heart*
> *Have I been speaking, and in my youthful mind.*

His youthful mind suddenly harmonized with his youthful body. As a matter of fact, poetry and the passion of living went together for Wordsworth. The sensual enjoyment of walks in the woods, of climbing, of rowing a boat, of seeking out the dark shadows of the night until fatigue made him rest under the nearest tree were all part of Wordsworth's poetic growth.

Years later, James Joyce said that a young writer needed silence, exile, and cunning. For William, the demands were otherwise. He needed a sense of place rather than exile; he needed the inspiration of creative friends rather than cunning, and, in all truth, he needed to speak, rather than remain silent. He could not resist reciting his poetry, even to his barber.

Joyce was a far lonelier man than Wordsworth, who was a great friend, a good husband, and an excellent family man. Both writers, however, had a sense of being apart, an aloneness peculiar to all writers. Henry James once advised a young writer, "there is one thing that, if you really intend to follow the course you indicate [the profession of letters], I cannot too emphatically insist on, there is one word, let me impress upon you, which you must inscribe on your banner, and that word is *loneliness*."

For William, that loneliness took the form of:

> *roving up and down alone*
> *Seeking I knew not what.*

Eventually, he was to find what he needed in the wildness of his own heart and his own landscape. Eventually, he would again find Dorothy.

❧ III ❦

Hawkshead

Fair seed-time had my soul, and I grew up
Fostered alike by beauty and by fear:
Much favoured in my birthplace, and no less
In that beloved Vale to which erelong
We were transplanted;—there were we let loose
For sports of wider range.

from: The Prelude
by: William Wordsworth

The steep crags always fascinated him. Even as a small child, he used to get a purchase on the rocks and pull himself up, bloodying his fingertips, tearing his old clothes, breathing heavily. Then he would climb, free and strong, finding some high point where he could look out on a cataract of water below, or on a still lake, or a valley of green. At school, in Hawkshead, he climbed all the time, sometimes far into the night, hunting bird nests, which, alas, was a favorite sport of the time. Sometimes he climbed lonely and free, wanting to be by himself; at other times he was surrounded by gay friends who dared each other to climb to higher rocks, higher crags.

One such trip was fraught with fear. William and his schoolmates John Benson, Tom Usher, and others, had started out, simply enough, to climb Yuledale Crags. They had seen ravens fly over the crags each day, and they thought there were probably eggs in their nests, or, perhaps, a small woodcock that could be trapped. The boys competed with one another, each climbing more recklessly.

William was frightened but determined not to show it. The crags were sharp, steep, and filled with crevices that could trap a wayward foot. On a high crag, John got caught. One boy after another tried to reach him or pull him loose, but it was obviously beyond the skill of twelve-year-olds; they had to send for help. Fear always sharpened William's perception and he was always to remember that climb: Benson, hanging, trapped on the crag, the others struggling to reach him, and the strange excitement of the moment of rescue.

The years at Hawkshead were remarkably vivid to him. Hawkshead was a market town that had once been a great cloth manufacturing center. In every cottage of the neighborhood spinning and weaving existed as home industries.

Every path in every road was an artery leading to Kendal, where the bales of cloth would be further processed. Each Monday morning, women would spread out huckster wares, and Wordsworth would often sit on a gray rock that served as one woman's shop, watching her spread her cylinders of carded wool.

The pack horses, laden with wool, or the ponies, bearing char pots, were figures in a landscape Wordsworth was never to forget. He was fascinated by "the pack people" who carried back packs of the charcoal that was made throughout the Lake District and then shipped to London.

School was of two kinds: one, the outside school of nature from which Wordsworth was always to take satisfaction; the other, the inside school, the Grammar School of Hawkshead, as remarkable as any of its time. It had been founded by Edwin Sandys during the reign of Elizabeth the First. William was enrolled in 1779, when he was just nine years old, and remained there as a student until June 20, 1787.

It was a custom of the time for the boys to board in the neighboring cottages, and William and his two brothers lived with Hugh and Ann Tyson, paying five guineas per half year.

School started out well. William discovered the great at-

21

traction of Latin and, at the same time, the pleasures of fishing with the village schoolmaster. But within the first few weeks he found the clothes of a drowned man beside one of the lakes—one of those experiences of horror that he remembered the rest of his life. Needless to say, the joy of fishing vanished.

Ann Tyson, his housemother, was a remarkable woman. She had, as had so many villagers of those days, a tremendous fund of stories and enormous patience with young boys. She allowed them freedom of the fields and of the crags. Night after night, in moonlit journeys, they would seek all the mystery and terror of the world hidden beyond the great oak trees.

Wordsworth often heard a "breathing" behind him, a kind of conscience that followed him wherever he went, particularly during the lamentable "bird-egging" expeditions. But most of the time he just felt pleasure and delight in the natural world around him. His blood began to flow with its own pleasure and he breathed with joy. Later he was to write:

> *Already I began*
> *To love the sun, a boy I loved the sun*
> *Not as I since have loved him, as a pledge*
> *And surety of our earthly life, a light*
> *Which we behold and feel we are alive;*
> *Not for his bounty to so many worlds—*
> *But for this cause, that I had seen him lay*
> *His beauty on the morning hills, had seen*
> *The western mountain touch his setting orb,*
> *In many a thoughtless hour. . . .*

He had an extraordinary feeling of being alive. "I was left alone seeking the visible world, nor knowing why." The world seemed unusually sharp and clear to him. Not only nature itself, but friendships appeared to be permanent.

22

His friends were numerous: strange solitaries like the packmen who lived in the town of Hawkshead, renting a little space, going through the dales selling needles and threads and household equipment, giving advice to the ladies of the cottages. Often an old packman could be persuaded to put down his wares and wander with the young boy over the dales, each one quiet, each carrying a different kind of pack, each taking tremendous satisfaction and pleasure in the other's company, and each with eyes particularly gifted for seeing everything beauteous: the meadow lily, a broken foxglove, a silent tree. "All that I beheld," Wordsworth said, "was dear to me."

As the years progressed, William discovered the world of poetry, and the new Gothic and romantic poets of the day: James Thomson, who spoke of the yearly seasons with enchanting clarity, and John Milton—"the superb Milton." Although books had been a familiar part of the Wordsworth home, there was a new sharpness to them. "Images, sentiments and words" almost became music and incense. Words began to take on, for William, a passion and a power.

At Hawkshead, mathematics also was stressed. It was, as it is today, a time of "new mathematics." At that time in the schools of southern England the classics were still taught almost exclusively with feverish concentration. In the northern schools, however, a new emphasis was being placed upon algebra and geometry. The seventeenth century had been the great age of mathematical discovery. Isaac Newton had made his mark, a mark that for William was to be continued at Cambridge University, where natural philosophy and mathematics sharpened the edge of his romantic temperament.

Other British boys would go to Cambridge having to study Euclid, algebra, and quadratic equations; but Hawkshead boys arrived there already advanced in hydrostatics, optics, and mechanics. The headmaster of Hawkshead had been a Cambridge man, and he taught his subject with pleasure and delight.

William's school books contained equations, but he soon had another, more important book: a manuscript book with a brown leather cover. He was beginning to write poems, and all the images that had been stored in his mind came into focus on paper. During his evening walks he had seen many things. Once, he saw the darkening boughs and leaves of an oak tree silhouetted against the sunset, and he tried to write about it, to shape it to the poet's pen.

"I recollect distinctly the very spot where this first struck me. It was in the way between Hawkshead and Ambleside and gave me extreme pleasure. The moment was important in my poetical history; for I date from it my consciousness of the infinite variety of natural appearances which had been unnoticed by the poets of any age or country so far as I had been acquainted with them; and I made a resolution to supply in some degree the deficiency. I could not have been at that time above fourteen years of age."

William wanted to capture the sharpness of nature, but he knew he had to do more than that; he had to consult both nature and his own feelings. He had to make nature, and his concept of it, express some of the torment, excitement, and immediacy of the sudden rush of emotions that sometimes overwhelmed him.

"Sounding cataracts" haunted him, he said, "like a passion." When he painted a landscape in words he was attempting to show the outlines of the landscape of the human heart. He knew he had received what he called the "precious gift" of poetry, but he knew, too, that his apprenticeship was just beginning.

When Wordsworth was fifteen, the Hawkshead School cele-

THE SCHOOLHOUSE, HAWKSHEAD

Illustration by Joseph Pennell

brated its two hundredth anniversary and he was asked to
write a poem. It is the first of his poems that survives—an
awkward, far too romantic piece that concludes:

> *To teach on rapid wings, the curious soul*
> *To roam from heaven to heaven, from pole to pole,*
> *From thence to search the mystic cause of things,*
> *And follow Nature to her secret springs.*

Even in these few lines, however, there is the sense of adventure, the suggestion that the creative spirit searches from
pole to pole as mysterious, solitary, and exciting as any explorer; that the world holds secrets only a poet, the greatest
of all adventurers, can reveal.

Small, daily adventures continued. Skating on a lake, the
boys would pause to watch the dusk fall and view the lights of
the cottages as they flickered on. In the evenings the boys
would sit around a fire, playing card games and smelling the
peat in the hearth. Always, there was Ann Tyson's superb
minced-meat pie and her warm affection. She was an influence that the motherless William was never to forget. He

now had the security of hearth and home that enabled him to develop a response to nature and beauty that was to carry him to the next period of his life.

When the Wordsworth boys arrived at Cockermouth for their annual vacation they found their father seriously ill. He had been lost in the crags while on a business journey and had found no shelter from the winter's cold. He died on December 30, 1783, leaving his five children orphans. At that time William was thirteen, Dorothy was just eleven years old.

❧ *IV* ❧

Do send a letter, do

Dear Child of Nature, let them rail!
—There is a nest in a given dale,
A harbour and a hold;
Where thou, a Wife and Friend, shalt see
Thy own heart-stirring days, and be
A light to young and old.

There, healthy as a shepherd boy,
And treading among flowers of joy
Which at no season fade,
Thou, while thy babes around thee cling,
Shalt show us how divine a thing
A Woman may be made.

from: To a Young Lady Who Had Been
Reproached for Taking Long Walks
in the Country
by: William Wordsworth

"It is terrible," wrote Dorothy, "to have neither a father, nor a home." She longed for both with a terrible anguish. Letters helped, and whenever Dorothy could, she stole time from the chores her grandmother always seemed to be preparing for her to write a letter to her friend, Jane Pollard. Sometimes such letters were filled with glorious trivia: gossip about the shops, whether or not she would buy a new bonnet, whether or not she would consider wearing high heels; but often there was a sad theme running through them: the loss of her parents and, perhaps even more painful to her, the loss of her home.

She could remember the distant castle of Cockermouth only vaguely, but there had been its green fields and water. There had been the feeling of running free, free as the natural world around her; the icy freedom of dipping bare feet into a river; the glorious excitement of throwing oneself upon the grass and looking up into the distant sky; the enchantment of hearing familiar voices, the kind voice of her mother and, although he has been away so much, the comforting voice of her father. Now Dorothy seemed to hear only her grandmother, muttering endlessly over needlework, trying always to find work for busy hands. There was to be no idleness in the house; even books were silly, and writing letters, of course, was ridiculous. Grandmother thought it better to mend a sock or a shirt, better to patch a sheet, than to waste one's time in a world of fantasy. Dorothy missed the conversation of her brothers: their endless talk and speculation and laughter, their stories of what they would do when they grew up, and the legends of the Border—the dreams of her own countryside.

Money! It seemed obsessive. She and her brothers were now just poor relations, and they were constantly reminded of their poverty. Their father's will was so involved and so complicated that little money was coming to them at all. Her grandmother muttered that they were not paying their way, and all that she, Dorothy, was good for was to mend a shirt, pull wool for the spinning, or be an unwilling ear to constant complaints. In the kitchen it was no better; she was little more than a servant, and she knew it.

"You would think," she wrote, "that a grandmother could feel more affection for a grandchild, particularly one who had lost her parents." It was easier for the boys. At least she hoped it was. They would be educated, of course, no matter what. But for a girl, what was there? Some letters, perhaps a journal in which she could put some secret thoughts, sometimes just a way of looking at life secondhand. She did not want to be a shadow; she did not want to be a household drudge. She wanted to be free.

Although Dorothy learned the things a girl was supposed to know about keeping a household, it was the outside world that always seemed to call her. She would give anything—yes, anything—to take her shoes off and leave this dark room and these dark village streets and run free once again—a gypsy, tanned, mysterious, part of the very earth around her.

The dingy, narrow streets of Penrith were filled, it seemed, with dirty, narrow people. They bored one another and themselves, they bored Dorothy too. Stealing time to write a letter was the best of her adventures. With the darning put away and the household tasks accomplished, she would go to the window, sit with a writing pad, and gaze out not upon the familiar scenes of her childhood, but upon the terrible reality of what her life had become. The Will! The Will! There had been so much difficulty about the will. Ever since her father had died his financial affairs had been hopelessly complicated. Although theoretically he had left the young Wordsworths well provided for, there was now, and would be for most of their lives, a lawsuit against Lord Lowther, who would try first one way and then another to avoid paying the amounts rightfully due the children by the terms of John Wordsworth's will.

Dorothy was glad that her oldest brother Richard was thinking of becoming a lawyer. Perhaps he would be able to extricate them from the confusion of legal matters. If the Wordsworths won the case, they would be assured of the money that would allow the brothers to do what they wanted, to become the men she knew they could be. John, of course, would go to sea. And William. . . . What would William become? Now she could only dream about her brothers; they could no longer talk and plan and discover the future together. In a letter to Jane, Dorothy voices some of her thoughts:

"They are just the boys I could wish them, they are so affectionate and so kind to me as makes me love them more and more every day. William and Christopher are very clever boys, at least so they appear in the partial eyes of a sister. No doubt I am partial and see virtues in them that by everybody else will pass unnoticed. John (who is to be the sailor), has a most excellent heart, he is not so bright as either Wm. or Christopher, but he has very good common sense and is very well calculated for the profession he has chosen. Richard (the oldest) I have seen, is equally affectionate and good, but is far from being as clever as William, but I have no doubts of his succeeding in his business for he is very diligent and far from being dull, he only spent a night with us. Many a time have Wm., J, C, and myself shed tears together, tears of the bitterest sorrow, we all of us, each day, feel more sensibly the loss we sustained when we were deprived of our parents, and each day do we receive fresh insults, you will wonder of what sort; believe me of the most mortifying kind; the insults of servants, but I will give you the particulars of our distresses as far as my paper will allow, but I cannot tell you half what I wish and I fear that when I have finished you will feel yourself almost as much in the dark as ever. I was for a whole week kept in expectation of my Brothers, who stayed at school all that time after the vacation begun owing to the ill-nature of my Uncle who would not send horses for them because when they wrote they did not happen to mention them, and only said when they should break up which was always before sufficient. This was the beginning of my mortifications for I felt that if they had had another home to go to, they would have been behaved to in a very different manner, and received with more cheerful countenances, indeed nobody but myself expressed one wish to see them, at last however they were sent for. . . ."

Dorothy, who loved to talk, now found herself taciturn. It was a great effort for her to remain silent.

"You cannot think how gravely and silently I sit with her and my Grandfather," she wrote about her grandparents, "you would scarcely know me, you are well acquainted that I was never remarkable for taciturnity, but now I sit for whole hours without saying anything excepting that I have an old shirt to mend, then, my Grandmother and I have to set our heads together and contrive the most notable way of doing it, which I daresay in the end we always hit upon, but really the contrivance itself takes up more time than the shirt is worth, our only conversation is about *work, work.* . . ."

Some of the work she relished, however. William had stayed with her for three weeks while she made him shirts for college. At least William, thank goodness, would be seeing something of the world.

When she dreamed, she dreamed that they would all be together again. Would it be the way it once had been? A house by a brook or by a lake, near a sweet mountain that one could look at or climb, the brambles catching in your skirt, the firs leaving little puffs of needles and thistles on your stockings. There seemed to be a thistle in her heart now, and her pain was like that thistle, scratching at her, tearing open again and again the wound she wanted to forget: the wound of being so terribly alone in the world. Good talk would help —it always helped—and these letters helped, too. She bent over her letter pad and wrote to Jane, with whom she could share all her thoughts. Didn't Jane understand that her letters were the happiest part of any day? Why did Jane take so long to write? Was it because Dorothy had so little time to write and Jane always waited for her letter?

"Oh Jane, Jane, that I could but see you! How happy, how very happy we should be! I really think that for an hour after our meeting, there would nothing pass betwixt us, but tears of joy, fits of laughter and unconnected exclamations, such as 'Oh Jane!' 'Oh Dolly!' It is now seven months since we parted, what a long time! We have never been separated so long for these nine years, I shall soon have been here a year. . . ."

It had been a terrible year; now it was a cold December. Dorothy was sixteen. She had nothing to look forward to. Her birthday would be Christmas Day, but her grandmother would ignore it. Oh, what grand days those Christmas birthdays had been in Cockermouth! The large roast beef on the great platter, the fat crackling, the fire in the hearth burning with joyous excitement, the laughter around the table, and then, in the evening, dancing. The delightful talk of her brothers, the strong voice of her father, and the distant voice, now a faint memory, of her mother.

She wrote another line to Jane: "Cast a melancholy thought upon your friend Dorothy." Then she added in a more girlish joy, "Do write to me very soon."

She thought of everything Jane was doing: her merry evenings and agreeable dances; she thought of Jane going out and walking. "It is a very fine morning. Most likely you are taking a walk up the bank." That steep hill ran a quarter-of-a-mile east, beyond Jane's house. It was partially wooded and Dorothy loved it. "I never go out but on a Sunday," she wrote, but even then her walks were not the same.

There seems to have been no Christmas letter from Jane, but Dorothy staunchly hid her disappointment:

"I had begun to be very uneasy, my dear Jane, on account of your long, long silence. I could not for a moment think you had forgotten me, no, Jane, I hope that will never be and that you will always remember with affection your Friend Dorothy, but I feared that you had put off writing to me from day to day till at last you knew not how to begin, you seem to fear lest I should be angry with you. Angry, my dear Jane, how is that possible when you can so well account for your silence?"

She continued her letter with the minutiae of the day's happenings but she could not prevent herself from falling into melancholy. "Oh Jane, you cannot sufficiently prize your kind parents. . . . How we are squandered abroad," she said, remembering a line from *The Merchant of Venice*. She and her brothers squandered like so many lost souls. She dreamed about how life would be: "I often wish," she wrote, "selfish as it may appear to you, that you, my dear Jane, were my Sister. I think how happy we should be! our fortunes would be but very small, but sufficient for us to live comfortably and on our Brothers we would depend for everything. I am now, alas! talking of the impossible, so I will drop the subject."

She wanted to send Jane a present, but she had little enough of her own and no money with which to buy a gift. She located a small thimble, packed it carefully, and sent it to her friend. As she continued her letter, she fingered a hand-kerchief once given to her by Jane who had marked it with her initials. "I have just this moment," Dorothy wrote, "pulled it out to admire the letters. Oh Jane, it is a very valuable handkerchief." There was not even any paper in the house for her to write on, and the grubby sheets she used for her letters needed an apology.

Sometimes she would manage to steal a little time before she went to sleep. Listening to her grandmother preparing for bed, Dorothy would realize with great pleasure that she would soon be quite alone. It was the time she enjoyed most, for she could then try to communicate with the people she loved, who seemed so far from her; she could fantasize about what the future would bring.

❧ *V* ❧

"My spirit was up,
My thoughts were full of hope"

My spirit was up, my thoughts were full of hope;
Some friends I had, acquaintances who there
Seemed friends, poor simple schoolboys, now hung round
With honour and importance: in a world
Of welcome faces up and down I roved;
Questions, directions, warnings and advice,
Flowed in upon me, from all sides; fresh day
Of pride and pleasure! to myself I seemed
A man of business and expense, and went
From shop to shop about my own affairs,
To Tutor or to Tailor, as befell,
From street to street with loose and careless mind.

I was the Dreamer, they the Dream; I roamed
Delighted through the motley spectacle;
Gowns grave, or gaudy, doctors, students, streets,
Courts, cloisters, flocks of churches, gateways, towers:
Migration strange for a stripling of the hills,
A northern villager.

from: **The Prelude**
by: William Wordsworth

"Sir, can you show me the way to Captain Robinson's?"

William waited patiently for an answer. It was October, 1787, and he was lost with his cousin, John Myers, in the great cathedral town of York.

"I'll show you if you give me sixpence."

Wordsworth handed a sixpence to the old man and was given the information. He turned to John and said, "Well, John, I can see that we are in Yorkshire now." Yorkshire inhabitants at that time had a reputation for being cautious with words, equally cautious with money, and very cautious with directions.

William and John, who were on their way to Cambridge University, found the Robinson house and were immediately welcomed by Captain Robinson, the husband of John's sister Mary.

"I hope, William, you mean to take a good degree," said Captain Robinson.

Wordsworth thought it over. "I will be either senior wrangler or nothing," he replied.

Years later, recalling the incident, Mrs. Robinson remarked, "And that's just what he was. He was nothing at Cambridge."

But on that October day Wordsworth's hopes were still high, though his plans were as uncertain as those of any young student leaving for college. Senior wranglers, or fellows of the college (in other words outstanding students), often were graduates of Hawkshead School. Certainly Wordsworth showed promise of becoming one. But in college he was to have one of those periods of indecision common to highly creative people.

Cambridge, in those days, was as beautiful as it is today. Just crossing Magdalene Bridge, which spans the "Cam," was enough to make Wordsworth remark, "My spirit was up, my thoughts were full of hope." But the academic world of late eighteenth-century Cambridge was far different from what one would find in universities today. It was a strange world for a young man with a North-country accent.

Indeed, at that time Cambridge was remarkably corrupt. In part, it catered to the very rich, who were to inherit titles (and who were called "Fellow Commoners"), and who therefore did not study but were highly accomplished in drinking and living a riotous life. A fellow commoner was described by a writer of that time: "Students (*a non studendo!*) who are in appearance the most shining men in the university. Their gowns are richly trimmed with gold or silver. These gentlemen enjoy the privilege of cracking their bottle and their joke, if they have one, in the Fellows Parlour, a combination room, where they are literally Hail Fellow, Well Met. It were almost endless to enumerate the privileges which these gentlemen enjoy by virtue of hereditary talents instilled into their breeches pocket."

Wordsworth's hereditary talents, of course, were those of his mind and his ability to perceive. His breeches contained little or no money; as a matter of fact, he attended Cambridge on a scholarship and, more than being on a scholarship, he was a sizar. At one point sizars had simply been servants to the fellows or the fellow commoners. They waited on tables and lived in the poorest rooms of the college, always wearing a distinctive gown and frequently eating leftovers from the fellows' tables. But some now bearing great names had been sizars at college: Isaac Newton for one, and Wordsworth's uncle, William Cookson, for another. Some sizars went on to head the university and to be people of merit. There were others, however, who remembered their college years as a time of great pain. Charles Lamb, who was later to be a friend of Wordsworth, had a schoolmate who was so disturbed by his role as sizar that he left Cambridge and went into the army. In the beginning, none of these rumors disturbed Wordsworth, or if they did, we have few records to prove this.

We do know, from his later poetry, however, that Cambridge did not live up to his expectations; that it fostered "forced hopes," and, in many ways, superficiality. Indeed, William was the young man in rebellion against the Establishment. As he looked upon himself he found:

> . . . *the inner pulse*
> *Of contemplation almost ceased to beat.*
> *Rotted as by a charm, my life became*
> *A floating island, an amphibious thing,*
> *Unsound, of spongy texture.*

At least, he thought, the floating island he had become could affix itself to the strong and flowering root of poetry.

It was at Cambridge that Wordsworth began his first long poem, "An Evening Walk." It is a sorrowful poem filled with melancholy details typical of a poetic period influenced by James Thompson's "Night Thoughts," and Milton's *Paradise Lost*—a period of lugubrious words and ornate styles.

Wordsworth planned what he called his own course of independent study, frequently to the great dismay of his relatives. He became fascinated with Italian, for example, and studied under a wonderful old man, Agostino Isola. Modern languages were rare in Cambridge in that day, and for a poor boy, as Wordsworth's relatives considered him, Italian would mean nothing. For a poet, of course, it was a great asset.

Some of the provinciality of eighteenth-century England made Wordsworth feel restrained, and his studies of other literatures freed him. But William could be extremely contrary. When a Master of St. John's died it was customary for undergraduates to write poems and pin them to the pall of the coffin. Wordsworth's Uncle William realized this was an opportunity for an ambitious, talented boy to make a name for himself in the college. But Wordsworth refused. He said later, "I did not . . . regret that I had been silent on this occasion, as I felt no interest in the deceased person with whom I had no intercourse and whom I had never seen but during his walks in the college grounds."

During vacations, William returned to Hawkshead, or, even more happily, visited Dorothy, now living with her beloved uncle, William Cookson, who, as a tutor to the Royal Family, had a keen interest in young people. When he married Dorothy Cowper, the daughter of a vicar, both Cooksons suggested that Dorothy live with them.

It was a happy change for her, and she was disturbed only by her feeling that William was too much the "floating island," that he did not know what he wanted to do. "I am very anxious about him just now," she wrote to Jane on April 30, 1790, "as he will shortly have to provide for himself: next year he takes his degree; when he will go into orders I do not know, nor how he will employ himself, he must, when he is three and twenty either go into orders or take pupils; he will be twenty in April."

But William was neither interested in going into the church nor in becoming a schoolmaster.

On July 14, 1789, an event occurred that was to be heard around the world, though it was little noticed in Hawkshead, where William was vacationing. The French mob's attack on the Bastille made a deep impression on Wordsworth. Although he was not identified with what was then called "the hotbed of radicalism" in Cambridge, his idealism was to break out later, when he went to France. He said in the great poem *The Prelude:*

> *. . . that unto me the events*
> *Seem nothing out of nature's certain course,*
> *A gift that rather was come late than soon.*

In other words, Wordsworth was not overly impressed by the French Revolution because he felt that freedom and the rights of man were common things. Anyone who walked through the dales of the Lake District knew that every individual should have his rights and his independence. Such people as the tyrannical Lord Lonsdale and the feudal barons of the North were not loved or appreciated in their own domains; they were loathed. Kings and nobles were ridiculous people. It was the aristocracy of the simple people that appealed to William and Dorothy Wordsworth, and William in particular, in the beginning, did not understand why the French Revolution caused so much excitement. He thought such a movement inevitable.

Cambridge was wild with the news of the uprising, and Wordsworth, continuing at college, began to pay less attention to the academic world in which he was immersed. He did not bother to take the required examinations, nor did he make an effort to write the exhortatory poetry in honor of the Revolution, so popular in Cambridge in those days.

Competition to become a senior wrangler was extremely strong. Where once William had been so fond of mathematics, he now turned his back on it. Although he did well in subjects in which he agreed to be examined, he was penalized for his neglect of others.

Cambridge, however, had opened the world to him. Now he wanted to see more of it. So in the summer of 1790 he went secretly, with his friend Robert Jones, to France and Switzerland. Wordsworth had to admit that his scheme was mad and impractical. He should have studied all summer. In September, William wrote Dorothy that he had given up all hopes for a fellowship:

"You will remember me affectionately and to my uncle and aunt: as he was acquainted with my giving up all thoughts of a fellowship, he may, perhaps, not be so much displeased at this journey. I should be sorry to have offended him by it."

Offence or not, William felt he was his own man. Let his family think what they might, he would spend some golden hours in France and then see the beauties of the Alps. He knew in his heart his talent was still in an unripe state, and no country could have been more stimulating to visit that summer than France. The whole world was mad with joy, and William was caught up in the excitement. As he and Robert walked the roads, at times almost penniless, they found "benevolence and blessedness, like a fragrance on the land." The Revolution was capturing Wordsworth's imagination.

William, however, remained shackled to an older age. His poems were still overburdened with the rich embroidery of an earlier period. His thoughts about the future were still confused. His present path, however, was clear. That summer,

41

in France and Switzerland, he seemed to know where he was going.

When the young friends landed in Calais on July 13, they immediately set out on a vigorous march, covering three hundred and fifty miles in two weeks. They explored the mountains and lakes of northern Italy and Switzerland, then bought a boat and rowed down the Cologne before returning to England on October 10. William wrote rapturously to Dorothy about what he saw:

"My Spirits have been kept in a perpetual hurry of delight by the almost uninterrupted succession of sublime and beautiful objects which have passed before my eyes during the course of the last month. . . . I have thought of you perpetually and never have my eyes burst upon a scene of particular loveliness but I have almost instantly wished that you could for a moment be transported to the place where I stood to enjoy it."

Wordsworth returned to Cambridge in late November, the last possible moment to prepare for his final examinations. He had had enough of college. Instead of studying during the last six weeks of his Christmas vacation, he went to the Cooksons' home, Forncett Rectory, to visit Dorothy. There he talked endlessly about the future and about poetry. Their conversations irritated his uncle enormously. What was this business about being a poet?

In January, 1791, William Wordsworth was awarded a B.A. degree by Cambridge. He received no awards and was, indeed, considered little more than a disappointment to his family. He was not a student; rather, he was a traveler, as he later admitted: "A traveler I am,/And all my tale is of myself."

His tale, for a while, would be not just of himself, but of a country's agony and of his passion for a woman.

❧ *VI* ❧

Terror

Domestic carnage now filled the whole year
With feast-days; old men from the chimney-nook,
The maiden from the bosom of her love,
The mother from the cradle of her babe,
The warrior from the field—all perished, all—
Friends, enemies, of all parties, ages, ranks,
Head after head, and never heads enough
For those that bade them fall.

from: **The Prelude**
by: **William Wordsworth**

"It was the best of times, it was the worst of times," Dickens was to write later.

Certainly to William Wordsworth, walking the streets of Paris in 1791, it seemed the worst of times. Terror was on the streets—terror and strange women, the *tricoteuses*. Clad in the worst of rags, demented and swollen with rage, they seemed bloodthirsty as they roamed the streets of Paris. Old ladies sitting at street corners, selling violets or brandy, would spit out the word "aristocrat," and those of noble birth who heard it were terrified. It was not a time for aristocrats in Paris. It was the time of Robespierre and the "Reign of Terror." The way of the aristocracy led to the guillotine.

Paris, at that time, numbered about 650,000 people, of which a large group consisted of derelicts and beggars, displaced persons unable to find jobs, who turned against the established authority for whom the Revolution had not meant civil liberty for all, but anarchy.

The *tricoteuses* sat in the courtrooms, some even sitting at the foot of the guillotines, knitting and shouting imprecations, laughing at those who were dragged, pushed, or carried off to be beheaded. Dickens, in *A Tale of Two Cities*, made one such woman, Madame Defarge, famous.

A historian of the time wrote: "I saw Paris in those days of crime and mourning. . . . From the stupefied expression on

44

people's faces you would have said that it was a city desolated by a plague. The laughter of a few cannibals alone interrupted the deadly silence which surrounded you."

Wordsworth walked the streets hearing the terrible sounds of the tumbrels, the straw-filled carriages that held the bodies of the victims of the Revolution.

One morning when the great square was filled, Wordsworth witnessed a sight that struck terror into his body. It was the execution by the guillotine, of A. J. Grosas. Wordsworth would dream about this event later, recall his ghastly fear, and try to exorcise it in his writing.

He knew his own life was in danger, and that he would have to leave Paris soon. In the meantime, he stood, almost glued to the cobbled streets, cragfast as he had been as a boy, watching the terrible scene before him.

Not just the Deputy, Gorsas, but twenty-one Girondists were jailed and executed that terrible October. As they were carted through the streets to the guillotine they sang the Marseillaise and they were still singing it as they stood on the high platform. The chorus grew slower, quieter, weaker, as the heads fell and the bodies were tossed into those terrible straw-lined carts. They died bravely, those Girondists, romantic figures of their own distorted ideals; ideals they had implemented in France, trying to turn her into an image of ancient Rome or Greece. This, then, was what had happened to the glory of the French Revolution!

Wordsworth was familiar with many Girondists. He was attracted by their philosophy and by the fact that many of them were delightful persons. Their name "Girondin" was derived from the fact that most of them came from the country around Bordeaux, where the Gironde River flowed sweetly through the rich valley. They sat on the left side of the House of Deputies in Paris, while on the right was another group, known as the Mountain, many of whom were considered nothing but cutthroats and thieves. These two groups, the Mountain and the Girondists, had been fighting for control of the Republic of France since the formation of the National Assembly in 1789. The Mountain appealed to the people of the streets: the criminals, and those who had little money and fewer cares. Now they had a leader, Jean Paul Marat, who said, "I am the rage of the people."

The struggle between these two groups culminated in the death of the Girondist faction in 1793. It was said that the night before the leaders were executed, they sat up all night in their crowded single cell talking seriously and philosophically about an afterlife, and about such people as Plato and Socrates.

They had erred by not really understanding the life of the streets. They wanted a republic, but they did not want to listen to the cries of the hungry. They did not know what the voice of anarchy really meant. They were great talkers; they dressed romantically in large, flowing coats; they had long hair, some of it cut in a Brutus fringe; they loved the Rome Wordsworth knew, the Rome of Plutarch, the Rome that fascinated a girl called Charlotte Corday, the Charlotte Corday who killed Marat in his bath; they spoke of the gods rather than of God, and they wrote and wrote. But too many of the words they used were empty.

"We don't want any more empty words," hungry people cried in the streets. Statesmen were needed, and the Girondists were not statesmen. Nonetheless, they were heroes to many: to poets, to writers who came after them. "To this devoted band of men whose whole career was justice and virtue, no one has dared to be contemptuous, and history on every side has left them heroes."

So, as heroes, Wordsworth saw them die on that terrible

day. Then, warned by his friends that his own life was in danger, he was spirited out of Paris, back to Orleans. The sights he had seen would continue to haunt him all his life. We know that William closely identified himself with the cause of the Girondists and that he was deeply shocked at the mass executions. He later told Thomas Carlyle, a historian of the French Revolution, that he had seen the execution of Gorsas.

"Where will it end, when you set an example of this kind?" William said to Carlyle.

The carnage of the later days of the Revolution almost turned Wordsworth into a pacifist. Violence would never do. In his "Ode" of 1815 he wrote:

> *Thy most dreaded instrument,*
> *In working out a pure intent*
> *Is Man-arrayed for mutual slaughter,*
> *—Yea, Carnage is thy daughter.*

The terror, too, had made it impossible for William to have any immediate contact with Annette Vallon, the French girl he had fallen in love with during an earlier trip.

❧ *VII* ❧

Between Heart and Heart

Strange fits of passion have I known:
And I will dare to tell,
But in the Lover's ear alone,
What once to me befell.

from: "Strange Fits of Passion Have I Known"
by: William Wordsworth

It was the first great love of his life—and the only one filled with an all-consuming passion.

William was by nature cautious. He had grown up in a part of the world where rock and tree, crag and cataract, were more overwhelming than the lives of the people. Now, in France, he discovered other passions: the passion of the Revolution itself, the passion of the movement of the people on the streets, and his own private passion for Annette Vallon. Even today, his first love, as he called it, remains a private passion, because there is a great deal about his relationship with Annette that is still a mystery.

We do not even know where they met. Was it in Orleans or in Blois? But meet they did, and that intensity of feeling Wordsworth was to later experience only in response to nature now settled on a young lady: twenty-five-year-old Marie-Anne Vallon, called Annette.

Born in Blois on June 22, 1766, Annette was the youngest of six children in a family of dignity and social standing. By the time she met Wordsworth, however, her father had died and her mother had remarried. Annette, like Wordsworth himself, was in that strange, in-between period of life when one tries to find his own identity. She knew only one method of self-discovery—and that was to be a woman. She loved William with unembarrassed passion, not thinking of him as a poet, but simply as a man, and later as the father of her child.

At twenty-one, Wordsworth, like many young men, was in a state of flux. When he arrived in Paris on November 30, 1791, he could not avoid seeing the effects of the French Revolution: Paris was a city "like a ship at anchor, rocked by storms." Still, he was politically ignorant. It was the sheer joy of being in Paris that delighted him. He was just a wanderer, a spectator. He recognized later that his first feelings were "as careless as a flower," and a hothouse flower at that—"while every bush and shrub, the country through, is shaking to the roots."

He was in Paris less than a week. Then he traveled down the beautiful Loire Valley to Orleans, which had long been a resort town for vacationing Englishmen but was so no longer. The Revolution had changed all that, and William found himself in a completely new environment.

He lodged in a pension that also boarded young cavalry officers. The officers had banded together into a "literary club," and they welcomed the young English poet. They were all aristocrats (the French cavalry at that time was made up only of young nobles) when the Revolution threatened: their hereditary honors would soon disappear. They talked and debated endlessly through the night, but William's French was inadequate to follow their arguments. Besides, he still did not comprehend how roughly the Revolution was tearing apart the fabric of the country. However, he did meet new people, particularly Paul Vallon, a young lawyer's clerk known for his wit and kindness. At first, the Vallons had supported the Revolution, but they were Catholics and the destruction of the nunneries and the edicts against Catholic doctrine made them change their views. They became increasingly Royalist in loyalty.

William was a democrat by nature. For him "wealth and

title were in less esteem / Than talents, worth, and prosperous industry." Still, the delightful Royalist Paul Vallon had become a great friend; and, more importantly, William had fallen madly in love with his sister Annette. They spoke different languages (Annette was to tutor him in French), had different religions, different political opinions. But nothing mattered; they were in love.

That spring was everything to him; it reminded him of tales from the *Arabian Nights,* of wonders he had never expected to find. "All the earth," he said, "breathed in one great presence of the spring."

He would walk by the house in which Annette lived, halting like Romeo beneath her chamber window. Merely entering her door revealed a different world to him—a world of enchantment. He said he was a man too happy for mortality; he acted as though such an experience had never come to anybody before. He did not realize he simply had fallen in love.

It was a love played out against the strange background of the Revolution. The intensity of the outside world, with all its confusions and bewilderments, matched the intensity of William's and Annette's private world. In the beginning, they thought they would marry, but, like many young men in love, Wordsworth was penniless. His relatives were still complaining he had no true career ahead of him. Annette had no money either, but walking was free. They walked in Orleans and in Blois, through the old neighborhoods Annette knew so well, past the convent in which she had grown up. They would talk of their happy, innocent years, which now had disappeared. They were lovers, sharing an "uneasy bliss," as Wordsworth called it, that was to haunt him for many years. They could not always see each other openly. He tried to find new outlets with new friends, men who had tossed aside their pasts and their families for the cause of the Revolution. Wordsworth often would go to patriotic clubs with Captain Michel Beaupuy, a Revolutionist, or they would take long walks while Captain Beaupuy preached the merits of the Revolution.

Beaupuy was a descendant of Montaigne. The captain was thirteen years older than Wordsworth and left a lasting influence on the younger man. Well read in philosophy and versed in French politics, he held opinions quite different from William's Royalist friends: the aristocracy must give up hereditary rights; poverty must be abolished; if Liberty meant Revolution, then the Revolution must continue. In *The Prelude* William was to extol Beaupuy:

> *Man he loved*
> *As man; and, to the mean and the obscure,*
> *And all the homely in their homely works*
> *Transferred a courtesy which had no air*
> *Of condescension.*

The Prelude is Wordsworth's great autobiographical work, but in it we find no mention of his great love affair with Annette; no mention of the fact that she was now pregnant. Wordsworth's reluctance to ever discuss his relationship with Annette in his work is understandable perhaps, but it does mean that an air of mystery will always hang over these years.

While William walked, he often must have been tormented. What was his next step? What should he do? There seemed no opportunity for them to marry. Annette finally decided to stay with friends in Orleans to await the birth of her child.

In the meantime, Wordsworth walked and talked. He wrote very little poetry now, but his letters show how desperately he wanted money and even guidance. Was he able to see Annette in Orleans? We do not know. He knew he should return to England, yet he lingered in Paris, and it was there he learned his daughter had been born on December 15, 1792. She was christened Annette Caroline Wordsworth, daughter of William Wordsworth, Anglois, and Marie-Anne Vallon. In the fashion of the day, Wordsworth, the absent father, gave legal power to a friend, André Augustin Dufour, who represented him.

Then the mystery deepens. William says he was dragged back to England by the chain of harsh necessity. Perhaps he planned to return to France immediately but could not. We do not know. It was a time of war, a time of trouble. Perhaps Wordsworth simply grew anxious. He was only twenty-one; Annette was four years older. She was a woman of great color, with a spirit of adventure even deeper than her lover's. Later, she would become a famous counterrevolutionary; in the meantime, she was only a woman in love with William, a woman who had borne his child, a woman who missed him.

The story of the strange love affair between Annette and William was, for many years, known only to the immediate members of both families and to a few of Wordsworth's very close friends. It was long after the early biographies were written that certain documents and lost love letters turned up, telling of the tragic tale.

William had confided in Dorothy and had then made a valiant effort to persuade his family to support his marriage to Annette Vallon. The odds were difficult: he was a Protestant, she a Catholic; he was an Englishman, she a French woman. William, however, seems to have been easily dissuaded by the negative attitudes of the respective families. Still, the two lovers thought they would eventually marry;

54

the pathetic letters Annette wrote during that time indicate this fact in every respect. Dorothy Wordsworth immediately became her confidant, and to her Annette wrote in French:

"I wish I could give you some comfort, but alas I cannot. I rather should look for it from you. It is in the certainty of your friendship that I find some comfort and in the unalterable feelings of my dear William's (sic). I cannot be happy without him, I desire him every day, but I shall have plenty of reasons for submitting to the lot which I must undergo. I often call to my aid that reason which too often is weak and powerless beside my feelings for him: no, my dear friend, he will never picture justly the need I have of him to make me happy; mastered by a feeling which causes all my unhappiness, I cherish always his dominion over me, and the influence of his dear love on my heart which is always concerned with him. His image follows me everywhere; often when I am alone in my room with his letters I think he has entered. . . . Ah, my dear sister, this is my continual state; emerging from my mistake as from a dream I see him not, the father of my child; he is very far from me. This scene is often repeated and throws me into extreme melancholy."

She wrote to William:

"My distress would be lessened were we married, yet I regard it as almost impossible that you should risk yourself if we should have war. You might be taken prisoner, but where do my wishes lead me?

"I speak as though the instant of my happiness were at hand, write me and tell me what you think and do your very utmost to hasten your daughter's happiness and mine, but only if there is not the slightest risk to be run, but I think the war will not last long. I should wish our new two nations to be reconciled, that is one of my earnest wishes, but above all find

55

out some way by which we can write to each other in case the correspondence between the two kingdoms is stopped."

Not only were the lovers parted; their two countries were now enemies. France had declared war on England on February 1, 1793.

Life became more difficult for Annette. Her family had been so shocked by her actions that they had placed her child with a wet nurse. Annette could not even see her. Now she had lost both William and her child, and her pain was intense. In a letter to Dorothy, she wrote, "I can assure you that were I happy enough to have my dear William journey back to France and give me the title of his wife I should be comforted. First, my daughter would have a father and her poor mother might enjoy the delight of always having her near. I should myself give her the care I am jealous to see her receive from other hands. I should no longer cause my family to blush by calling my daughter my Caroline. I should take her with me and go to the country. There is no solitude in which I should not find charm being with her."

Time passed, but the pain was not lessened. In another letter to Dorothy she wrote:

"Often when I'm alone in my room with his [William's] letters I dream he is going to walk in. I stand ready to throw myself into his arms and say to him: Come, my love, come and dry these tears which have long been flowing for you, let us fly and see Caroline, your child and your likeness; behold your wife; sorrow has altered her much; do you know her? Aye by the emotion which your heart must share with her. If her features are altered, if her pallor makes it impossible for you to know her, her heart is unchanged. It is still yours. Know your Annette, Caroline's tender mother . . . Ah, my dear sister, such is the habitual state of my mind but, waking from my delusion as from a dream, I do not see him, my child's father. He is very far from me. These transports occur again and again, and throw me into a state of extreme dejection."

We do not know how many such letters exist. Unlike Wordsworth, Annette wrote copiously. All her letters are emotional, as well they might be, but never does she seem to have approached him as a poet; to have recognized that he, too, was struggling for some identity; that not only was a war being waged in the outside world, but in William's own soul as well.

Perhaps his memory of the streets of Orleans and that intense feeling he had experienced there had dissipated. Perhaps he simply longed for quiet, for peace, for some understanding of how he could redirect his poetry, of how he could serve another mistress: his poetic muse. Annette and William were never to lose contact with each other, but that fire—the fire they both felt—was to burn in other areas of their lives. Annette, curiously enough, would become more politically oriented. She would be well known as an intriguer against the new regime. A report of the secret police carried the following paragraph:

"The Vallon sisters as well as their sister Madame Williams have always been known as friends and abettors of the royalty. They have a brother who is under supervision in my department and who was for a long time imprisoned in the Temple Premise on account of journeys he had made into foreign parts with Madame de Bonneuil. The woman Williams, particularly, is known as an active intriguer. The police commissary of Blois assures me there are no suspicious meetings in that house. As I have only today returned to my department I cannot give more positive information in that matter, but I am going to arrange for a watch to be set on them which will let me know all that is done at their house."

William returned to London in December, 1792. He stayed with his brother Richard, who was much against William's new "radical" ideas and equally against his new radical friends, such as Mary Wollstonecraft, later to be the author of *The Vindication of the Rights of Women,* and William Godwin, author of *An Enquiry Concerning Political Justice.*

Not only was political justice seeking a new freedom, but so were the "new women."

VIII

Extraordinary Women

Her voice was like a hidden bird that sang;
The thought of her was like a flash of light,
Or an unseen companionship; a breath
Of fragrance independent of the wind.

from: "On Nature's Invitation Do I Come"
by: William Wordsworth

Although William was a wanderer, Dorothy still had to stay at home. She was now living in Forncett, where she was as happy with her uncle and his new bride as she had been unhappy with her grandmother. She was now writing, with great pleasure, to her friend Jane Pollard.

"My room," she wrote, "is one of the pleasantest in the house, some of the views are beautiful. . . . I arise at six every morning and, as I have no companion, walk with a book till half-past-eight if the weather permits. If not, I read in the house. Sometimes we walk in the morning, but seldom more than half an hour just before dinner. After tea we talk together until about eight, and then I walk alone as long as I can in the garden. I am particularly fond of a moonlight or twilight walk. It is at that time that I think most of my absent friends."

It was an interesting age for women—truly an extraordinary age—and many exceptional women were emerging, as Dorothy was—still almost in a chrysalis, but finding her way —and attempting to achieve a form of expression.

Isolated as she was, Dorothy still met a number of famous men and women. William Wilberforce, for instance, a British abolitionist, was a visitor at Forncett.

The talk during these visits was often of the new world that was coming. In this new world, many women were to have an important place. In the late Victorian period women would become more repressed, less individualistic, but at this time women could very distinctly be their own persons. Not only would Dorothy's name live as long as her brother's, both as his inspiration and as a brilliant diarist in her own right, but other friends, other women of their acquaintance, such as Mary Lamb, who, with her brother Charles, was to become an influential writer, would open new fields.

There were new ideas in the land; for example, that women might be able to work. Women began to look clearly at the miserable state of society—the poverty and the disasters of the early Industrial Revolution, which was creating havoc in the countryside and in the cities. Edmund Burke said it was an age distinguished by having produced extraordinary women, and certainly that was true.

In the early nineteenth century, bluestocking clubs, groups of influential women, sprang up in London. The women in these intellectual clubs wore blue stockings and tried to prove that women were the equal of men. The bluestockings became known all over England. Although neither Mary Lamb nor Dorothy Wordsworth considered themselves bluestockings, they did train themselves to think and write clearly. It was a period in which women were beginning to publish. Jane Porter produced a book entitled *The Scottish Chiefs,* which became famous all over England; Maria Edgeworth wrote *Castle Rackrent.* Other female writers, such as Fanny Burney and the wonderful Jane Austen, were putting the mark of a woman's sensitivity on literature. A few years later, Mary Wollstonecraft (whom William Godwin was to marry) published a famous book called *Vindication of the Rights of Woman.* Her daughter Mary would marry Percy Bysshe Shelley, and as Mary Shelley, be remembered for that classic novel *Frankenstein.*

61

If a woman did not choose to write, she could teach. Dorothy had a small school, and similar schools flourished throughout England.

Women were rebelling; bold thinking among them was rife in the land. Mary Lamb, for example, who made her living by sewing, wrote a famous essay on needlework to try to emphasize the economic stature of women.

Nonetheless, many famous women lived in the shadows of men: Mary in the shadow of Charles Lamb, Dorothy in the shadow of William. But for Dorothy it was only a public shadow; in private she was more. She knew how important she was to her brother, how deeply his work relied upon her, how it would always rely upon her. She would be his eyes and ears; she would transcribe his poems and listen to them; she would walk with him and talk with him. She was to be—as she dreamed even in those years of separation—more than a sister. She was to be a companion in his creativity. If she could not be with him now, she would travel the same path as he in the future.

In the meantime, she spent that summer of 1793 writing personal criticism of a small quarto volume of poetry that had just been published in London. It was called *An Evening Walk* and was, as the author, one William Wordsworth wrote, *An Epistle, in Verse. Addressed to a Young Lady, from the Lakes of the North of England.* The young lady, of course, was Dorothy.

That same summer, the small volume was read by another emerging poet, Samuel Taylor Coleridge, who immediately recognized Wordsworth as a poetic genius—a genius whose words and images were "all aglow." Surely their paths would soon cross.

❧ IX ❧

"To be young was very heaven"

How oft, amid those overflowing streets,
Have I gone forward with the crowd, and said
Unto myself, "The face of every one
That passes by me is a mystery!"

from: The Prelude
by: William Wordsworth

London! William did not want the serenity of the country. The streets of France, he wrote sometime later, had opened up "dangerous passions within," and so, upon his return to England, rather than seeking the countryside that was to nurture him throughout his life, he turned instead to London—the great London—that had always been a place of romance to him.

Wordsworth remembered that once, when he had been a schoolboy, a student friend had visited London, and upon his return young William tried to discover how his face was changed by the trip. Something had to be changed; such an experience had to leave its mark on everyone's face. Surely London was a fairyland. For a boy growing up in the North, it was a place of adventure, of marvelous happenings: Lords in ermine coats, the King in his palace, the sights and the sounds—particularly the articulate music of the bells—and the strange anonymity of the streets, "strangers, not knowing each the other's name."

As a boy, William had heard all about London: street-lamps that dimmed the stars, magical fireworks for festive occasions, the ever-present street activity. Then there was the Thames River; the awesome dome and whispering gallery of St. Paul's; the giants of Guildhall; the graying statues and monuments; men on horses; and always—always—the endless stream of moving things.

London was certainly the place for a young man with passion in his veins; with his eyes and ears imaginatively perceiving strangers, and the wonderful variations of color, light, form, and even the deafening din of the city; constantly watching the trade signs in front of all the eighteenth-century shops, great swinging signs with huge letters, all of these attracted him.

Then there were the "rarey shows," as William called them. He tramped endlessly through the streets of London, coming abruptly upon these street shows, which might feature a company of dancing dogs, or a camel with a monkey on its back, or a minstrel band. He would walk in secret places: in private courts and hidden alleys "gloomy as coffins"; he would linger on street corners hearing all the cries of London: "Strawberries, strawberries for sale!" "Fresh mint, fresh mint!" "Hot cross buns, hot cross buns one a penny, two a penny, hot cross buns!"

William would walk into the wide main streets and see the strange, solitary people, as isolated as those he had known in the dales: a lonely man sitting in the sun; a cripple stumping by on his arms; a beggar passing his hat in the crowd. Here, on the streets of London, were persons from all the world: Swedes and Russians, Frenchmen and Spaniards, some even from remote America. "It was," said Wordsworth, "the absolute presence of reality."

Often William would go to Sadler's Wells, where years later there would be a famous theater. In his day, however, it was still half rural, with clowns and harlequins to delight children and men, both young and old. At other times, William went to the theater to see the great actress Sarah Kemble Siddons perform. He became joyously excited by the drama, as he was by the pleasure of the marketplace and the agitation of political gatherings. All this, to him, was London. "The huge, fermenting mass of humankind," he called it, "a picture

in relief, as one might see a figure upon the mountaintop."
"I said unto myself the face of everyone that passes by me
is a mystery." Sometimes he would be overwhelmed by a sudden, unforgettable impression: a blind beggar, for example,
who had propped against his chest a paper explaining where
he came from and who he was.

All London seemed to impress itself upon his eye, upon
his ear, upon his consciousness. When darkness came, he
would see the moonlight and the stars, shining over the empty
streets; in the deep of night he might hear the muttering of
some old woman; but he noticed that no one would turn
around, no one would look. At dawn, sometimes, the streets
were mobbed; perhaps because of a fire on a corner, or an
execution, or perhaps just because of preparations for the
great excitement of St. Bartholomew's Fair. As the day moved
on, the noise from the fair became barbaric and infernal.
Everything was motion, color, shape, sight, sound. Monkeys
dangled from poles, children whirled on their roundabouts;
there was the sound of the kettledrum and the hurdy-gurdy.
The puff-cheeked trumpeter and all the strange characters of
the fair made St. Bartholomew's unforgettable: the horse of
knowledge; the pig that knew how to read; the stone eater;
the ventriloquist; each vying for the attention of one vast,
milling mob of men, women, and children.

Wordsworth was to catalogue the joys and miseries of London in the seventh book of his poem *The Prelude*. He had
returned from Paris, stimulated but emotionally exhausted.
He still did not know what he planned to do. He was eager
to see Dorothy, and yet he lingered. His family was against
him, shocked by his affair with Annette, bewildered by his
inability to choose a career for himself. They made no effort
to see him.

William's absence pained Dorothy. She longed for him,

BARTHOLOMEW FAIR

and he, as his letters showed, longed for her. Dorothy was
now twenty-one. She felt she had spent too much time without her brother and was eager to see him. Sometimes she felt
impelled to write Jane in an attempt to explain her feelings.
One summer evening she wrote:

"I am willing to allow that half the virtues with which I
fancy him endowed are the creation of my Love, but surely
I may be excused! he was never tired of comforting his sister,
he never left her in anger, he always met her with joy, he preferred her society to every other pleasure . . . he had no
pleasure when we were compelled to be divided . . ." And
then she went on to describe William at that period of his
life: "In the first place you must be with him more than
once before he will be perfectly easy in conversation; in the
second place his person is not in his favor, at least I should

think not; but I soon ceased to discover this, nay I almost thought that the opinion which I first formed was erroneous. He is, however, certainly rather plain than otherwise . . . but when he speaks it [his countenance] is often lighted up with a smile which I think very pleasing, but enough, he is my Brother, why should I describe him? I shall be launching again into panegyric."

William, in London, walking the streets, and Dorothy, in Forncett, taking care of her aunt's children, both wished for the same thing: some little cottage where they might live together sharing peace and companionship. William would write poetry, Dorothy would take care of him; they would live in utter contentment. Once he wrote to her:

"How much do I wish that each emotion of pleasure and pain that visits your heart should excite a similar pleasure or a similar pain within me, by that sympathy that would almost identify us when we have stolen to our little cottage. I am determined to see you as soon as I have entered into an engagement, i.e., as a tutor. Immediately I will write to my uncle that I cannot think of going anywhere before I have been with you. Whatever answer he give I will certainly make a point of once more mingling my transports with you. Alas, my dear sister, how soon must this happiness expire, yet there are moments worth ages."

They planned to meet in Halifax, outside the prying eyes of their relatives:

"Oh my dear, dear sister, with what transport shall I again meet you, with what raptures shall I again wear out the day in your sights. I assure you so eager is my desire to see you that all obstacles vanish. I see you in a moment, running or rather flying to my arms."

On some days, William and Dorothy imagined that Annette and her child would come and they would all live happily in that cottage; on other days they would ignore all thoughts of Annette and think only of their own future.

William had by now published *An Evening Walk,* and Dorothy, who was a stern critic, commented:

"The poems contain many passages exquisitely beautiful, but they also contain many Faults, the chief of which are Obscurity, and a too frequent use of some particular expressions and uncommon words, for instance moveless, which he applies in a sense if not new, at least different from its ordinary one; by moveless when applied to the Swan he means that sort of motion which is smooth without agitation; it is a very beautiful epithet but ought to have been cautiously used, he ought at any rate only to have hazarded it once, instead of which it occurs three or four times."

Correction was always painful to William, but he gave the utmost care to Dorothy's criticism. Suddenly turning to prose, he wrote a bitter attack against the Bishop of Landoff, who had preached as a member of the Establishment and for the British world as it was. William was against monarchy, which, he felt, allowed the social ills of the times to go uncorrected. His essay argued against war and poverty. It was, for its day, intensely radical. The times were not favorable for its publication, and he was warned that he might be in great danger if he made known his quarrel with such a famous Bishop.

Frustrated, Wordsworth looked for something to do. In the summer of 1794, his path crossed that of a schoolmate from Hawkshead, William Calvert. Calvert's brother Raisley, not quite twenty, had a small amount of money in trust, and the old school friend suggested that Wordsworth might be a proper tour companion for the young man. William accepted the invitation.

Raisley and William began their journey on the Isle of Wight and proceeded to Spithead. From there, they traveled across the superb Salisbury Plain. Unfortunately, their "whiskey," or traveling carriage, broke down, and the two friends separated, Raisley taking the horse and going northward, and William simply taking "a pair of stout legs" and traveling through Salisbury into North Wales. It was a sudden change from London, and William once again found himself isolated, but he felt a rapport with this natural environment.

The trip resulted in one of his famous early poems, "Guilt and Sorrow," one of the first poems in which he tried to understand the social factors of contemporary English life.

As William journeyed, he saw what the Industrial Revolution was doing to the countryside. Every village was changing. The early part of the eighteenth century in England has been called a kind of golden age. This was the era of rural England: of the great roast beefs, the great cheeses, the great holidays; an era of a kind of hushed peace that supposedly exists just before some important event occurs, changing all aspects of life. In our own twentieth century the period before World War I was called a golden age; the eighteenth century was just such a period—before the Industrial Revolution. The century moved on, however, and between 1760 and 1815 rural England was transformed. This was the time of the Enclosure Acts, in which the fencing in of open-field areas, so maintained since the Middle Ages, forced a new way of living in the villages.

There had never been a true golden age anywhere; there had always been some degree of poverty and misery in the world. Nevertheless, the early eighteenth century had been an affluent period during which trade grew rapidly and the population, fortunately, grew slowly. With the growth of trade came the demand for home manufacturing. In rural cottages, women and children did carding and spinning. Corn was cheap, the standard of living was rising, yet there were always some who were poor. They would squat on the town commons, or eke out a living by poaching or by cutting wood and turf.

At the end of the eighteenth century, agriculture was still a great industry. But at the time of Wordsworth's birth, two important changes were taking place: the population was beginning to increase, and trade was weakening.

Wordsworth could sense this change, and he grew more eager than ever to find a rural home. He yearned to express the deeply felt response to nature reawakening within him. If only he could share a secluded, rural life with Dorothy and some congenial friends!

Then, as so often happened to Wordsworth, opportunities presented themselves. The first was a result of tragedy. Young Raisley Calvert, who had always been frail, was discovered to have tuberculosis. He was obviously dying, and William stayed with him in the Lake District, comforting him until his death in January, 1795. Raisley was impressed not only by William's kindness, but by his obvious dedication to poetry, and by William's confidence in his own ability to contribute something to the world. At his death, Raisley bequeathed Wordsworth £900, truly a windfall for an impecunious young poet.

William then went to London to stay with a friend he had met in Cambridge, a young widower, Basil Montagu, with a son named Basil Montagu, Jr. Montagu was concerned about the welfare of his child, who in 1795 was four-years-old and needed not only country air but also the care of a sympathetic woman. Why not Dorothy? Why shouldn't William and Dorothy look after young Basil? They should have fifty pounds a year for his upkeep and a rent-free home, Racedown Lodge, in Dorset, where they were to live for two years.

William and Dorothy were delighted to have the opportunity to live together. Basil—although "he lies like a little devil," said Wordsworth—was often a real pleasure. The senior Montagu, however, was often short of funds, and William's new inheritance was frequently tied up. Consequently, they lived very simply, from their garden and orchard. Tea, claimed Wordsworth, was their only luxury.

The true luxury for William lay in his opportunity to write poetry in leisure and solitude. "We are both" wrote Wordsworth to a friend, "as happy as people can be who live in perfect solitude. We do not see a soul." The secluded months that followed led him to write, "Our present life is utterly barren of such events as merit even the short-lived chronicle of an accidental letter. We plant cabbages; and if retirement in its full perfection be as powerful in working transformations as one of Ovid's gods, you may perhaps suspect that into cabbages we shall be transformed."

Instead, he was transformed into a productive poet. He revised his great poem *Salisbury Plain,* began a dramatic tragedy, *The Borderers,* and wrote such poems as *The Old Cumberland Beggar* and *The Ruined Cottage.*

Dorothy was happy. "Racedown was the first home I had," she recalled later; "I think that it is the place dearest to my recollections upon the whole surface of the island."

The little the Wordsworths needed was well supplied. Sometimes they were lonely, but that loneliness vanished with new friendships.

On a trip to Bristol, William met two exciting new friends. They were both young radicals, both poets, and, in fact, brothers-in-law. They had planned an ideal society, a community—they called it a "pantisocracy"—to be founded in America, but as with so many such dreams, the idea foundered.

The first friend was Robert Southey, born four years after

ROBERT SOUTHEY AT FORTY-ONE

William, in 1774. "Very pleasant in his manners," thought
Dorothy and William, "and a man of great reading in old
books." The other was a very "noticeable" man indeed, "a
noticeable man with large grey eyes."

His name was Samuel Taylor Coleridge. Those large grey
eyes fastened on Wordsworth and his poetry. "Giant
Wordsworth," said Coleridge, "God love him."

As for Dorothy, said Coleridge, she was an exquisite sister.
"She is a woman indeed; in mind I mean, and heart. . . . In
every notion her most innocent soul beams out so brightly.
Her eyes watchful in minutest observation of nature."

Dorothy's eyes, and William's, were sharp in other directions. Now that they had found Coleridge—they must not lose
him. They found a house near where Coleridge lived at the
foot of the Quantock hills for a small rental. They gathered
up young Basil, and took off for one of the greatest creative
experiences of all times.

73

❧ X ❧

That wonderful man,
Coleridge

I was a Traveller then upon the the moor;
I saw the hare that raced about with joy;
I heard the woods and distant waters roar;
Or heard them not, as happy as a boy:
The pleasant season did my heart employ:
My old remembrances went from me wholly;
And all the ways of men, so vain and melancholy.

from: Resolution and Independence
by: William Wordsworth

"We are," said Coleridge, "three persons with one soul." So they were: Dorothy, William, and Samuel Taylor Coleridge. No matter that Coleridge had a wife, Sara. Often pregnant and uncomfortable, she did not enjoy the endless walks of the three friends or their constant stream of conversation, which was as colorful and as sparkling as the waterfall in Alfoxden Park, near Coleridge's home in Nether Stowey. Nor could Sara share in the creative rush of genius that enveloped Dorothy, William, and Coleridge as though it were some powerful, invisible friend. Besides, Samuel was a "character," and had been, he said, since the age of eight. Though they may make fascinating friends, "characters" usually make poor husbands.

Coleridge used to delight William and Dorothy with the story of his early life. His father before him, as Coleridge was about to do, had made the world his confidant. The elder Coleridge was a minister who "knew much Latin, Greek and Oriental languages."

Samuel, born on October 21, 1772, was one of thirteen children. His father, nonetheless, always had time for him, and just as people would talk about him, they talked about his father.

The elder Coleridge was often absent-minded, and there were delightful stories about his escapades. Once he appeared at a dinner with his shirttail hanging out. He immediately collected himself and, behaving as mannerly as possible, tucked the shirttail into his trousers—only to discover that he had also inserted the trailing skirt of a lady in a white dress sitting next to him. On another occasion, he was to go on a trip. Dutifully, he promised his wife he would wear a clean shirt each day. When he came home, his family was dismayed to find he had followed instructions, but he had put on a clean shirt over the dirty one he had worn the previous day—and he hadn't even noticed.

Samuel Coleridge had been raised in a house of talkers. He and his father talked about everything and, in fact, young Samuel was less comfortable with his many brothers and sisters. He explained to the Wordsworths that as a young boy he had been fretful and timorous and that his only pleasure was reading books. His aunt had kept an "everything-shop," one of those eighteenth-century stores that sold a little bit of everything, and there he found colorfully covered little books of great tales: *Jack the Giant Killer, The Arabian Nights, The History of St. George, The Famous History of the Seven Champions of Christendom.* "Give me," he cried in later years, "the works which delighted my youth! Give me *The Arabian Nights' Entertainments* which I used to watch till the sun shining on the bookcase approached and glowing full upon it gave me the courage to take it from the shelf."

Much that Coleridge read frightened him, and at night he would be haunted by spectral images. Sometimes he was so disturbed by his reading that his father burned the books. "So I became a dreamer," he said, "with an indisposition to all bodily activities; and I was fretful and inordinately passionate, and as I could not play at anything [his health was poor] and was withdrawful, I was despised and hated by the boys. Because I could read and spell and had, I may truly say, a

memory and understanding that forced me into almost an un-
natural rightness, I was flattered and wondered at by all the
old women. And so I became very vain and despised most of
the boys that were at all near my age. . . ."

When Samuel was nine his father died, and he felt a loneliness that was to haunt him throughout his life; a loneliness
the Wordsworths understood so well. Samuel was sent to
Christ's Hospital School. He was then just beginning to write
poetry, but of a particularly doggerel kind:

> *Oh Lord have mercy on me,*
> *For I am very sad*
> *For why, Good Lord,*
> *I've got the itch,*
> *And Eek, I've got the tad.*

"Tad" was a slang word for many of the itches boys had
because of the poor diet at the school. Coleridge was eloquent
about his schooldays:

"I was a poor, friendless boy; my parents, and those who
should have cared for me, were far away. Those few acquaintances of theirs, whom they could reckon upon being kind to
me in the great city, after a little forced notice, which they
had the grace to take of me on my first arrival in town, soon
grew tired of my holiday visits. They seemed to them to recur
too often, though I thought them few enough. One after another they all failed me, and I felt myself alone among six
hundred playmates. Oh the cruelty of separating a poor lad
from his early homestead! The yearnings which I used to have
towards it in those unfledged years! . . . The warm, long
days of summer never return but they bring with them a
gloom from the haunting memory of those whole days' leave,
when, by some strange arrangement, we were turned out for
the livelong day, upon our own hands, whether we had friends

to go to or none. I remember those bathing excursions to the New River which Lamb recalls with so much relish, better, I think, than he can, for he was a home-seeking lad, and did not care much for such water-parties. How we would sally forth into the fields, and strip under the first warmth of the sun, and wanton like young dace in the streams, getting appetites for the noon; which those of us that were penniless (our scanty morning crust long since exhausted) had not the means of allaying, while the cattle and the birds and the fishes were at feed about us, and we had nothing to satisfy our cravings; the very beauty of the day and the exercise of the pastime, and the sense of liberty setting a keener edge upon them! How, faint and languid, finally, we would return toward nightfall to our desired morsel, half rejoicing, half reluctant, that the hours of uneasy liberty had expired!"

His worst troubles with young friends passed, and he became very capable of making extraordinarily close friends, ones he would keep all his life. Coleridge had an amazing gift for friendship, though his friends were often sorely tried. He borrowed money, squandered affection, had a terrible intensity in all his relationships, and yet he was loved by many. He used to say that he jumped over "the stile of friendship" the way one would jump over a stile in an open field. Friendship was not enough for him; he jumped from friendship into intimacy. Women, as well as men, found him extremely attractive, and Dorothy Wordsworth certainly was more than a little in love with him for many years.

By the time he went to Cambridge University, he was fascinated with words, poetry, science, girls—with the whole world. But poor Samuel always managed to get a cold and always worried about it. "Cambridge," he said, "is a damp place, the very palace of the winds: so without very great care one is sure to have a violent cold. I am not, however, certain that I do not owe my rheumatism to the dampness of my rooms. Opium never used to have a disagreeable effect on me."

He had discovered—not an unusual experience in those days—that opium would alleviate his various aches and pains. It was, of course, to become the pernicious habit that eventually destroyed his life.

By the time he left college, he knew only one thing: he did not know what he wanted to do. The Wordsworths understood this period of vacillation but could not quite comprehend the bohemian life style in which Coleridge indulged during and after his college years. In London, during one of his self-awarded vacations from college, he had barely any money and gave what he did have to a horde of beggars.

Once, he was utterly desperate. What was he to do? While strolling, he passed an army recruiting office and went in. He was a sorry-looking recruit. The general in charge stood before him and said, "Your name, sir?"

"Comberbacke, sir," replied Coleridge. It would never do for his family to know he had gone into the army.

"What do you come here for, sir?"

"To be a soldier, sir."

"Do you think you can run a Frenchman through the body?"

"I don't know, sir, as I never tried, but I'll let a Frenchman run me through the body before I'll run away."

"Good enough," said the general, and left the office.

"Comberbacke" made a rather extraordinary soldier, and legends about him flourished in later years. He used to tell the Wordsworths a story about the time he was a sentry at an officers' ballroom. Two officers passed, intently discussing the Greek dramatist Euripides. "Comberbacke" could not keep quiet. "Excuse me, sir," he said, "but those lines are not quite accurately quoted. Besides, they are not from Euripides; they're from the second antistrophe of the *Oedipus* of Sophocles."

"Who the devil are you?" said one of the men. "Old Faustus grown young again?"

"I am Your Honor's humble sentinel."

"Damn, sirs," said the officer, "the fellow must be a gentleman, an odd fish; not an odd fish, but a stray bird from Oxford or Cambridge."

Certainly Coleridge was acting like a stray bird. He disliked soldiering intensely, and did nothing to deter his brothers from trying to obtain his release from the army. On April 10, 1794, a man called Silas Titus Comberbacke was discharged from the service as insane, and Samuel Coleridge went lumbering back to college. Confined to college for a month, he settled down—but not for long! He was ready for new experiences, to meet new friends. One he met was Robert Southey, who was just as great a talker as Coleridge. He could talk anyone into anything, it was said. Thin, arrogant, with icy eyes and stiff movements, he was a fighter. He had been dismissed from school because he had written an article against corporal punishment, which was flagrant in those days.

Besides Southey, Coleridge met Charles Cottle, the publisher; he met those great philanthropists, the Wedgewood family; and he met the beloved Charles Lamb. Still, it seemed to him he had spent his life thus far looking for the ideal friends. At last he found them: William and Dorothy.

❧ XI ❧

Channels for Streams

She welcomed what was given, and craved no more;
Whate'er the scene presented to her view
That was the best, to that she was attuned
By her benign simplicity of life,
And through a perfect happiness of soul,
Whose variegated feelings were in this
Sisters, that they were each some new delight.
Birds in the bower, and lambs in the green field,
Could they have known her, would have loved; me-
     thought
Her very presence such a sweetness breathed,
That flowers, and trees, and even the silent hills,
And everything she looked on, should have had
An intimation how she bore herself
Towards them and to all creatures.

from: **The Prelude**
by: **William Wordsworth**

Some books are meant to be fondled as well as to be appreciated, to be looked at physically as well as to be emotionally understood. Some books are small enough to hold in the hand, to take on a picnic, to put in a pocket, to amble with through the woods. One such book is an Oxford Classic called *The Journals of Dorothy Wordsworth*. It is one of the great literary treasures of all times.

It was on January 20, 1798, in the town of Alfoxden in the Quantock Hills, that Dorothy Wordsworth began the journals that comprise her book. She settled down and wrote with a steady hand, not at all worried about her handwriting. Now she was in direct communication with the natural world around her. She wrote: "The green paths down the hillsides are channels for streams, the young wheat is streaked by silver lines of water running between the ridges, the sheep are gathered together on the slopes. After the wet, dark days, the country seems more populous, it peoples itself in the sunbeams."

For the next few days, devouring the landscape with her eyes, she wrote brief excerpts of her impressions and thoughts in her little notebook. She noticed that great trees near enough to the sea had a feathery sea-green moss upon their trunks. The sea itself, when she walked to it late in the afternoon, was calm and blue, and the sand jutted out into tongues. She and William walked in the evening, the red sunset exciting them. The winter had released the sound of the sea that, in the summer, had been muted by the many trees. Now that the trees were barren, the roar of the water continuously came to their ears.

The cry of the birds was gone, the crickets were silent; there was only the music of the ocean itself. Late each afternoon she and William would begin a walk that continued into the cold, clear evenings. The sea was ever-changing; blue yesterday, it was gray today. By late January, the bright sky of autumn became just one ominous cloud. Often Dorothy and William would walk up the rugged sheep trails and sit in the sunshine. The bells of the sheep were the only sounds other than the distant water. Sometimes they saw an old woodsman walking along the road with his laden pony, the wood on the animal's back spangled with dewdrops. Close to the shore the woods were like skeletons.

They walked in the evening, watching the moon break through the overhanging oaks. There were still leaves on some of these trees, but all had turned a withered yellow. By the end of January the storms had come—great, raging storms—and William would climb to the top of a hill to see the heavy, black clouds racing shoreward across the water.

Sometimes he would stay up late at night and call his sister out into the garden. He would point to the moon, suddenly very colorful, and the stars shining with a strange glow.

Each day, as Dorothy recorded her observations, her eyes seemed to grow sharper. It was not that their life was always interesting. Sometimes the walks were tiresome, but her eyes became trained. On rainy nights, the sky scattered with clouds and the wind and rain beating at their faces, Dorothy and

William would walk along the hawthorned hedges, touching the tops with their fingers, watching the raindrops break into spots of water.

By the first of February the weather had turned fiercer. Now the trees, as well as the sea, roared. Where there had been slight sound the month before, they now seemed to be surrounded by it. The wind so cut into their faces that they often had to seek shelter. But then, nature could change; the next day could be delightful. A redbreast might start to sing; there might be young lambs in a pasture, and Dorothy might watch them staring at her with their black, glaring eyes, their large heads shaking with some kind of arrogant knowledge of nature itself.

On February third, a beautiful, mild morning, she and William walked with Coleridge. That evening Dorothy wrote in her *Journal*, "I never saw such a union of earth, sky and sea." But there was more than a union of nature. One of the great friendships of all times, one of the greatest creative unities, among Dorothy Wordsworth, William Wordsworth, and Samuel Coleridge, had come into being. It was, indeed, a merging of earth, sky, and sea; a meeting of personalities that was to have a profound influence on English literature.

Samuel Coleridge, in June, 1797, had written about Dorothy: "Wordsworth and his exquisite sister are with me. She is a woman indeed; in mind I mean, and heart; for her person is such that if you expect to see a pretty woman, you would think her ordinary: if you expected to see an ordinary woman, you would think her pretty! But her manners are simple, ardent, impressive. In every motion her most innocent soul beams out so brightly, that those who saw would say 'guilt was a thing impossible in her.' Her information various. Her eye watchful in minutest observation of nature; and her taste a perfect electrometer."

William himself copied the first paragraph of her Alfoxden journal into his own notebook. During these months her observations, her ability to see the subtlest beauties, the "perfect electrometer" of her taste as Coleridge called it, were to inspire both men. One of the great Wordsworthian critics, Ernest de Selincourt, has said, "Dorothy Wordsworth is probably the most remarkable and the most distinguished of English writers who never wrote a line for the general public."

She had never truly thought of being an author. She once said, "I should detest the idea of setting myself up as an author." But she had the ability to record the immediate scene with the freshness and flavor, the preciseness and taste that proved she was instinctively a great writer. The journal she began on that January day has left us all in her debt.

❧ XII ❧

The Ancient Mariner

A narrow girdle of rough stones and crags,
A rude and natural causeway, interposed
Between the water and a winding slope
Of copse and thicket, leaves the eastern shore
Of Grasmere safe in its own privacy:
And there myself and two beloved Friends,
One calm September morning, ere the mist
Had altogether yielded to the sun,
Sauntered on this retired and difficult way.
——Ill suits the road with one in haste; but we
Played with our time; and, as we strolled along,
It was our occupation to observe
Such objects as the waves had tossed ashore—
Feather, or leaf, or weed, or withered bough,
Each on the other heaped, along the line
Of the dry wreck.

from: Poems on the Naming of Places
by: William Wordsworth

Once, as the Wordsworths and Coleridge walked across a hill and saw the darkening late afternoon sky oppress the landscape, they sensed they were passing through a spectral world. They talked of the local folklore. Here, at Watchet, there was a strange story of a ghost ship that had landed at Minehead. When boarded, it was found to have neither captain nor crew. It was a deserted ship that might have been captained by a spirit or crewed by shadows! Each year, in May, the legend of that ship is perpetuated by the Watchet community in songs and plays. "Where there were stories," said Coleridge, "there was always poetry," and deep in his mind the idea for his great poem, "The Ancient Mariner," was born.

Coleridge and the Wordsworths were both familiar with the old sea tale of "The Flying Dutchman." The variations on this theme of a deserted ship appear in the literature of all countries. In the story familiar to Coleridge, the captain of the original ship was a Dutchman with a belief in nothing—except his own power at sea. He believed in neither the gods nor the saints. Once, near the Cape of Good Hope, a great storm arose. The sailors aboard the ship began to pray, begging the captain to put into shore. But the mad captain laughed at the storm, mocked the praying sailors, and stood squarely on the deck, defying Providence and the tempest to take his ship. As he stood there, one of the great storm clouds above him opened, and a celestial figure descended. The crew shook in terror, but the captain did nothing. He stood there laughing, staring straight ahead. The figure spoke to him: "You are mad, captain. You have the madness of a man who seeks too much power. You are mad and, more than that, you are impolite."

"Get off my ship," the captain replied. "Get off my ship or I will blow your brains out." Then he took a pistol and shot the figure. But the shot boomeranged. It could not kill the spirit; instead, it pierced the captain's own body. Blood began to pour from his hand. He jumped at the cloudlike ghost, ready to strike him, but his arm dropped uselessly at his side.

The figure spoke to him once more: "Now there is a curse upon you, captain. A curse not even time can heal. You will sail forever. Never will you come to port or harbor, but you will sail on the ocean forever drinking only bitter gall, and just as you may never dock, you may never sleep. You will grow sleepy with the terrible fatigue of the years, but all you will do is watch. You will watch forever. If you close your eyes just once, a sword will pierce your body. You who have tormented your own crew and have laughed at the dangers of the water, you are now the evil genius of the sea. You will be a ghost of the sea; you will go through all latitudes knowing no one, talking to no one, never resting, never finding fine weather. All who see you and your ship shall have misfortune."

And so the Flying Dutchman sails on. In the eighteenth century this was one of the favorite stories of the sea. Old diaries tell us that sailors often thought they passed such a phantom ship at night; that some had actually tried to touch it. Once a hand was extended, however, the ship would vanish. Such ships have appeared in many literary works:

Captain Marryat wrote a famous book, *The Phantom Ship,* Wagner, an opera called *The Flying Dutchman,* and our own Longfellow based a poem on this famous legend. The story could not help but inspire Coleridge to attempt to write a poem. The legend fascinated him, as it did Dorothy and William.

In those ambling walks they spoke, William, Dorothy, and Coleridge, not only of such legends but of all the great Elizabethan tales of adventure. These tales stimulated a great renaissance of poetry in Queen Elizabeth's time, and they supplied rich material for a writer. There were newer tales, too, that William, Dorothy, and Coleridge had read since they were children, tales of exploration and discovery: tales of strange voyages to the northwest and the attempts to reach Asia; tales of great sea dangers; tales of the arctic and its icy waters breaking up ships; and tales of the strange birds, and the flora and fauna that were seen on many sea voyages. Wordsworth told Coleridge he had been reading Shelvocke's *Voyages* and had run across a description of a great bird, the albatross.

Could they not collaborate, William and Coleridge wondered, on some poem that would provide enough money for a great walking trip for the three of them, a journey during which they could just talk of poetry, eat simple food, stretch their legs, and be together as one. Could Coleridge and Wordsworth really collaborate? They were so very different. But Coleridge was enthusiastic. Indeed he could. His friendship with the two Wordsworths had opened up a great new field of creativity for him. Yet how would they proceed?

All poets are ancient mariners, navigating the strange eddies of their unconscious, not knowing whence the images they will use must come. There is a famous book called *The Road to Xanadu,* by John Livingstone Lowes, which is one of the pioneer works to attempt an explanation of the images of Coleridge's poems, particularly "The Ancient Mariner" and "Christabel," written when the poet was a close companion of the Wordsworths. But even a whole book cannot explain a single poem. There is something beyond literary references and images that inspires such a work. There was, between Wordsworth and Coleridge, a closeness of relationship; a curious sense of guilt that both poets shared; a heady ferment of excitement, stimulated by walking and talking together in an intimacy that neither had known before. Coleridge had always found himself, as Wordsworth had, a lonely, solitary man; he was his own figure of the ancient mariner, sailing in fiery seas or arctic water, caught between passion and expression, between intellect and heart.

Coleridge and Wordsworth had tried to collaborate once before, on a poem to be called "The Wanderings of Cain." The former, excited by the idea, promptly did his share, but William could do nothing. Instead, he sat staring at a blank piece of paper. But this evening, talking of this new ballad together, Wordsworth contributed several important suggestions. He wrote later:

"Much the greatest part of the story was Mr. Coleridge's invention; but certain parts I myself suggested, for example, some crime was to be committed which should bring upon the old Navigator, as Coleridge afterwards delighted to call him, the spectral persecution, as a consequence of that crime, and his own wanderings. I had been reading in Shelvock's *Voyages* a day or two before that while doubling Cape Horn they frequently saw Albatrosses in that latitude, the largest sort of sea-fowl, extending their wings 12 or 13 feet. 'Suppose,' said I, 'you represent him as having killed one of these birds on entering the South Sea, and that the tutelary Spirits of these regions take upon them to avenge the crime.' The incident was thought fit for the purpose and adopted accordingly. I also suggested the navigation of the ship by the dead men, but do not recollect that I had anything more to do with the scheme of the poem. . . . We began the composition on that, to me, memorable evening. I furnished two or three lines at the beginning of the poem, in particular:

> " 'And listened like a three years' child;
> The Mariner had his will.' "

But again the collaboration did not work. The phantasmagoria of the poem—its marine images, its deep passion— was beyond Wordsworth or, quite differently, not in the manner in which he wanted to work. He let Coleridge complete the poem alone, and in 1798, one of the great works of genius in English literature was completed: "The Ancient Mariner." As Dorothy says in her journal, on the evening of March twenty-third, Coleridge brought to her and William "his ballad finished." It was "a beautiful evening," she reported, "very starry, the horned moon." What is so interesting is that during this period Dorothy's journals constantly refer to images and descriptions similar to those that Coleridge incorporated in his poem. Their minds were so attuned, so alike, their conversation so omnipresent, that it is difficult to say whose images were whose. Here was a companionship that had to continue.

If Wordsworth and Coleridge could not write together, perhaps they could publish together. Both wanted to travel to Germany but could do so only on the money they might receive for their poems. Therefore, they would attempt to publish one volume, called *Lyrical Ballads,* with poems by both. It would be published anonymously because as Coleridge pointed out, "Wordsworth's name is nothing, and mine stinks."

Lyrical Ballads was to become one of the great experimental publications of the period: it combined the "supernatural" with the everyday world; it had the voice of two great artists; it had a youthful, joyous spirit that has rarely been surpassed.

Unfortunately, the book did not sell well. But, undaunted, the three friends managed to scrape together a small sum of money that enabled them to make their trip to Germany. Thinking it unwise to subject young Basil Montagu, Jr. to such a trip, the Wordsworths returned him to his father. Then, "on foot, per wagon, per coach, per postchaise," they made their way to the harbor of Yarmouth.

❧ *XIII* ❧

*I travelled among
unknown men*

I travelled among unknown men,
  In lands beyond the sea;
Nor, England! did I know till then
  What love I bore to thee.

'Tis past, that melancholy dream!
  Nor will I quit thy shore
A second time; for still I seem
  To love thee more and more.

Among thy mountains did I feel
  The joy of my desire;
And she I cherished turned her wheel
  Beside an English fire.

Thy mornings showed, thy nights concealed
  The bowers where Lucy played;
And thine too is the last green field
  That Lucy's eyes surveyed.

from: "I Travelled Among Unknown Men"
by: William Wordsworth

The only one at the railing of the steamer was Coleridge. Ever since the preceding morning, Sunday, September 16, 1798, William and Dorothy had been below in their cabins, violently ill on this, their first important trip together. Seasickness seemed to be omnipresent; the packet in which they were traveling rose and fell as did the ocean. "Indeed," wrote Coleridge later, "everyone was seasick." As he described some of the passengers in a letter to his wife, he put an asterisk in front of the names of those who were only slightly ill and a dagger in front of those who were violently ill. He was delightfully proud that he himself was the only one on board who saw the English shore recede from sight.

At night, he said, the North Sea was a "noble thing" with white clouds and stars of flame that danced and sparkled. Occasionally, a star would seem to detach itself from the others and disappear into the night. Sometimes Coleridge looked into the water at what appeared to be stars. The sea glittered with what the sailors called "fish spawn" (actually phosphorescent algae that shone in the night). As Coleridge contemplated the ocean, he was besieged immediately by homesickness and by a desire to see the faces of his wife and children. He had two young sons, and their faces came to him vividly in a flash of lightning. Hartley was his special favorite; Berkeley had been only a babe when Coleridge left on this journey, hoping to make a better living for his family. Those faces, streaking across his eyes that night, were never to be quite the same. Little Berkeley contracted smallpox and Sara Coleridge was to write shortly, "The dear child is getting strength every hour; but when you lost sight of land and the faces of your children crossed you like a flash of lightning, you saw that face for the last time." Indeed, Coleridge was not to see that disfigured face at all, because by the time he returned from Germany, Berkeley had died.

Coleridge urged William and Dorothy to get up from their cabins, which were, in those days, miserably close, with bad air that smelled of nausea and bilge water.

There were not many people aboard the packet, despite the fact that Germany was one of the few countries to which the British could travel safely now that Napoleon Bonaparte's army had taken control of most of western Europe. Scandinavia, however, was still free, and there were Swedes and Danes aboard the ship who befriended Coleridge. They called him "Doctor Theology" because of his black suit and black stockings.

The trio reached the mouth of the Elbe River shortly after one of the sailors gave a cry that land had been sighted. Dorothy dressed herself and went up on deck. She clung to the railing, trying to control her sickened mind and body, but both seemed to defeat her. Even at anchor the ship rolled unmercifully. Amidst the strange languages of the Danes and the Swedes, she stood on deck trying to orient herself.

There was land indeed: a farmhouse, a few cattle, a haystack, a windmill. She began to wonder why they were making this trip, a thought that has come to every traveler who discovers some of the privations and suffering he must endure to satisfy what Wordsworth called "that wild wandering spirit in all of us." Had they come here to learn German? Had they

99

come to be with Coleridge? Had they been talked into the trip? Well, it did not matter at the moment; just the sight of a haystack and cottage was a good omen. Dorothy felt well enough to have a cup of tea; the moon came out, and for a moment she was happy.

Now the question was: How would they get to Hamburg? It would cost only another ten guineas, the captain said. Both Coleridge and Wordsworth, who had been obliged to borrow just to make the trip, shuddered at the idea of further expense. However, their share came only to half a guinea, because one of the Danes was lavish in his contribution. They finally arrived in Hamburg, only to find it an ugly city; one, Coleridge said later, that "stinks in every corner." The hotels were abominably crowded. That first night they slept, all three, in one large, filthy room. For food, there were some extremely bad cucumbers, and some very cold, fatty beef. In the morning, after they paid their bill, it was discovered that they had been cheated. Although they did find cheaper, more comfortable quarters, their trip had not started well.

Perhaps it would be better if they separated, Coleridge going on to the town of Ratzeburg, William and Dorothy staying in Hamburg for a while and then, gypsy fashion, going where they would, picking up the language as they went, looking at the countryside. Not having as much money as Coleridge, or the desire to immerse themselves in the city life of Hamburg, Dorothy and William chose to go to the more scenic locales of southern Germany. Here they would be able to learn the language in order to translate German books, a task that was then quite profitable. Also, they would be able to live cheaply in the tranquility of the Alpine region.

After separating from Coleridge, the Wordsworths settled in the town of Goslar, an old city more than a little decayed, resting at the foot of the Hartz Mountains. Lodgings were reasonably comfortable, breakfasts were sketchy—bread and apples—but as the year moved on and the cold grew worse they were grateful for whatever meager habitation they had. William worked hard, but not at learning German. For some reason the language eluded him. French came easily to him. It had been the language of his young revolutionary spirit and of his own deep desire for Annette. German was something else again, forcing him to withdraw into himself, into his own language, into his own past.

When he wrote now it was not about the German scenery or his daily life in that country, but poems that were haunted, beautifully, by his own past—by the hills and mountains of Cumberland. When Coleridge wrote of how much he enjoyed skating in Ratzeburg, William remembered the skating parties of his own youth, one of the boyish pleasures he had enjoyed around the Lake District. He began to think of those early years and of a biographical poem that he might compose. Wasn't all of youth a prelude? A beginning? He started to outline such a project, writing of how he sailed as a boy, of how he and his friends "nutted" in the north of England.

Communication with his homeland was almost impossible. Letters were either lost or greatly delayed. But even the letters from Coleridge, still in Germany, were few and far between. The Wordsworths longed for Coleridge. Why didn't he come? Soon, they would have to return to England.

Often, William walked in the moonlight wrapped in a black jacket and a great fur coat, which he had bought to ward off the intense cold. Dorothy thought he looked extraordinarily handsome. At other times, he simply kept to his room, saying each day that they would leave Goslar. Where could they go? The roads were atrocious; all the carts that could carry them and their meager belongings (mostly books) were completely uncovered, offering no protection from the snow. It was, indeed, one of the most severe winters of the century.

Christmas was the coldest day they had ever known. Even as they moved around in their lonely room they had to wear coats. It was certainly no time to leave. They must wait until the spring, when they could walk. Then they could see the rest of Germany and perhaps learn the language more satisfactorily; they were not learning it in Goslar. They kept too much to themselves; they were too isolated; they had no money to entertain and consequently were rarely invited out. In addition, it was awkward for a man and woman, as sister and brother, to travel together in Germany. They were a strange combination, and the petty tradespeople of the town did not understand them. Their landlady had five children, and both Dorothy and William thought she cheated them. They could, however, understand why: she needed the money. Still, they were hurt and bewildered, as foreigners often are in a strange country.

Coleridge, meanwhile, was leading a high life and, indeed, was much lionized. His German became so skillful that he could immediately translate his poems into the language. His quick wit and conversational ability brought him the friendship of counts and countesses.

The social life was not for the Wordsworths. They dreamed of being together at some place less cold, less miserable. Goslar may once have been the home of emperors, but now, Dorothy muttered, it was nothing but the home of "gross souls." There was one person they loved—one kind, dear creature—but he was miserably deaf, and their conversation was limited. They had to get out of Goslar.

By the end of February, their bags long since packed,

Dorothy awakened to see the sun shining, for once, into the garden. Now they could leave!

They started to walk through a pine forest, past tiny waterfalls (Coleridge called these small cataracts, kittenracts). The landscape reminded William of a miniature version of the Alps. He and Dorothy walked all day and in the evening found, in the midst of the Hartz Forest, an inn that pleased them.

In the morning, as they left, the mountains seemed to be following them, surrounding them. There was Brocken, the glory of Germany, the Mont Blanc of the Hartz Forest. Impressive as it was, Dorothy preferred her own mountains in the north of England. But at least the days were clear and bright, and they could continue their journey. At night they could expect only a hard bed, a heavy frost, cold beef, and the usual cabbage. Occasionally they would stop in one spot long enough to receive a letter from Coleridge, and they considered it their greatest joy.

Eventually, the Wordsworths caught up with Coleridge in Göttingen, but after a short visit (they didn't even stay overnight) William and Dorothy moved on. Their visit with Coleridge only increased their melancholy. Surely they must all live near one another when they returned to England, and surely they must live in the Lake District of their native land. All one could ask was for one's countryside, a place to write, and a decent library. They longed for home—for England. Later Wordsworth was to write:

> *I travelled among unknown men,*
> *In lands beyond the sea;*
> *Nor, England! did I know till then*
> *What love I bore to thee.*

It was essential that Dorothy and William return home.

THE MILL AT AMBLESIDE
A favorite haunt of the Wordsworths

Illustration by Joseph Pennell

❧ *XIV* ❧

Dove Cottage

Embrace me then, ye hills, and close me in.
Now in the clear and open day I feel
Your guardianship: I take it to my heart;
'Tis like the solemn shelter of the night.
But I would call thee beautiful; for mild
And soft, and gay, and beautiful thou art,
Dear valley, having in thy face a smile,
Though peaceful, full of gladness. Thou art pleased,
Pleased with thy crags, and woody steeps, thy lake,
Its one green island, and its winding shores,
The multitude of little rocky hills,
Thy church, and cottages of mountain stone
Clustered like stars some few, but single most,
And lurking dimly in their shy retreats,
Or glancing at each other cheerful looks
Like separated stars with clouds between.

from: "On Nature's Invitation Do I Come"
by: William Wordsworth

Throughout their lifetimes, Dorothy and William were to take many walks, but none was as important to them—as colorful or as meaningful—as the one they began in December, 1799. In a way they felt they were walking into the future. It was a cold, frosty morning, but the sky in the east was a delicate pale orange. It was a beautiful morning—they were going home.

True, Dorothy had never seen the cottage, but William had told her about it. It had once been an inn, called The Dove and Olive Bough. Downstairs there was a large room (large at least by the standards of the region) some sixteen by twelve feet wide—a dark, stone-floored, oak room in which the windows were paned with diamond-shaped glass that caught the sun. The kitchen, William explained, was in wretched shape, as was the bedroom, also stone-floored. The fireplaces smoked dreadfully, and all the rooms had to be curtained. Where would they put William's three hundred books? Where would his study be? Was there a garden? Dorothy would plant one with peas, French beans, spinach, broccoli, and kidney beans. But it was winter now; spring planting was far away. Now they could only plant their dreams.

After his return from Germany, William had gone on a walking tour in this very area with his brother John, a sailor

who for the moment was on leave, and with Coleridge who
had returned to England in July, 1799. William hoped to
build a house in this vicinity, borrowing some of the needed
money from John and earning the rest himself. A good house
could certainly be had for a small sum. Unfortunately, the
plan fell through. Finances, as always, were difficult to arrange.
Instead, William leased the cottage that has been known ever
since as Dove Cottage.

William and Dorothy started the three-day journey to their
new home from Sockburn-on-Tees, where they had been staying with their friends, the Hutchinsons, since returning from
Germany.

Traveling on horseback both day and night, they finally
stabled the horses and set off on foot. The cottage was in an
area of waterfalls, each one more spectacular than the other;
"a countryside," said Wordsworth, "that had been laid out by
some giant gardener." Everything was vast and grand and
seemed in a state of cultivated wilderness. Walking was not
easy; the roads were frozen, and darkness fell rapidly. William
and Dorothy looked forward to each morning, and when a
thin layer of snow had covered the ground, they discovered
that it helped; one could keep one's footing more easily in
snow than on ice. They would stop by every stream, look at
every wood-covered bank, and walk into every delightful
meadow, soft and comforting to their feet after rocky river-
beds and ledges of waterfalls.

On the coldest day they faced, they walked twenty-one
miles in a state of strange exhilaration. If they ran across a
farmer with his cart they might hitch a ride, but more frequently they enjoyed being alone, walking on deserted trails,
searching out one waterfall after another. Dorothy thought
the tumbling water looked like congealed froth, frozen and
white with snow. They would try to find a dry spot, such as

a cave in the rocks, from which to watch the dazzling colors that appeared as the icicles dispersed the rays of sunlight. Always they were aware of the sky. There were scenes worthy of the *Arabian Nights,* and it was difficult to pull away, to move on to the next inn—to move on to Dove Cottage.

On December 17, 1799, they opened the door of their new cottage to discover cinders still glowing in the smoking fireplace. Dorothy wrote later, "We have returned to our native mountains, there to live." They were both filled with great satisfaction.

There was so much to do: curtains to make, rooms to be painted. Their excitement quieted only when they both developed bad colds. But, dripping nose or not, Dorothy still washed and ironed, papered, cooked, and cleaned. No matter what they were doing there was always time for a walk and time to talk to old Mr. Sympson, a former vicar who was now some eighty years old; to Molly Fisher, "Old Molly," the woman who helped in the house for two hours a day; to her brother; indeed to all the cottagers of the neighborhood. But as soon as the first curtains were up, the first wall papered, the first room painted, they longed, as usual, for Coleridge. Not only for Coleridge but for their brother John, who with his quietness, sincerity, and affection for both William and Dorothy was like a vine from which the flowers of their spirit might take nourishment and blossom.

John came in January. He was waiting the arrival of his ship, *The Earl of Abergavenny,* which he would captain. He was a sailor not only in reality but in heart, "shut within himself," as his brother and sister said. He had been that way since childhood. John was so cautious of making friends that even William and Dorothy seemed a bit of a threat to him. When he came to the door of Dove Cottage he twice put his hand upon the latch, and twice turned away without the

DOVE COTTAGE

courage to enter. Finally, he sent word that he was at the local inn, and his brother and sister rushed to greet him.

"He was an unexpected delight," they said. "A friend who had a perfect sympathy with nature and with them." "John was," said William, "of all human beings whom I ever knew the man of the most rational desires . . . the most perfect self command. He was modest and gentle, and shy even to disease. . . . In everything his judgments were sound and original; his taste in all the arts, music and poetry in particular . . . was exquisite; and his eye for the beauties of nature was as fine and delicate as a poet or painter."

John enjoyed fishing in the lakes and loved to go out in the evening to look at the clear moon. So, for that matter, did William, who often persuaded Dorothy to accompany him. For two months the three Wordsworths lived ideally, working a little in the house, sitting around the fire in the evening, listening to William's poetry. Then, in February, Mary Hutchinson came. John was delighted with her. "He was the first," she said, "who led me to everything that I love in this neighborhood." To John she was a friend; to William she was more. He had known her through childhood, and now that he was beginning to feel he should settle down he thought of Mary as more than a friend. Surely, she was the woman he would marry.

Of course William was frightfully poor. John realized his plight. "I will work for you," he said, "and you shall attempt to do something for the world. Could I but see you with a green field of your own and a cow and two or three other little comforts, I should be happy." He knew William had great genius and he was willing to do everything he could to support his brother.

Perhaps some of the joy and satisfaction of the period was due to the fact that the Wordsworths had been without a home for so long. Speaking of John after his death, Dorothy said, "He loved this fireside, he paced over this floor in pride before we had been six weeks in the house, exulting within his noble heart that his father's children had once again a home together."

In any case, their happiness was such that they wrote few letters and Dorothy did not even keep a diary.

With the spring, things changed. The landscape beckoned and William and John responded by visiting the Hutchinsons. On May 14, they set off with "cold pork in their pockets." As the first leaves and bulbs sprang to view, Dorothy had a desire to put her pleasure and delight—and her loneliness —on paper. She could hardly bear her brothers' absence. The lake that had looked so beautiful now appeared dull and melancholy; the sounds on the shore, which before had been music, now had a dead, dull sound. She would walk by herself, kicking the stones, as a child might do at the shore. She would walk through the woods seeing yellow flowers and grassy-leaved, rabbit-toothed, white flowers, wild strawberries,

geraniums, violets, anemones, primroses. Despite the green-
ness of the land and the beautiful views, life seemed tiresome.
She decided to write another journal—this one for William
and John to enjoy when they returned from their journey.
Like Dorothy's first journal, this "Grasmere Journal" is one
of the great chronicles of literary history. Dorothy entered
everything that happened to her, all her emotions and all her
wishes in the journal. If she was depressed, she would write
awhile and her sadness would depart. At night, she would
write and then go to bed. It did not matter that tomorrow
would be a dull morning.

Each day she would walk to Ambleside, hoping to receive
a letter, but there was none—only a newspaper—and she
would cry in disappointment. Even a letter from Coleridge
did not help. The beauty of the area was almost more than
she could bear by herself. Each day she recorded in her journal "no letter, no William." Coleridge must come to keep her
company. She must find him quarters. Some have felt that
Dorothy and Coleridge were lovers, but her journal says nothing about this. It is only the birds that she talks about, "the
little birds busy making love and pecking the blossoms and
bits of moss off the tree; they flutter about and about and
thrid the trees as I lie under them. Mary went out for tea, I
would not go far from home, expecting my brothers. I ram-
bled upon the hill above the house, gathered wild thyme,
took up roots of wild columbine." But on the following day
there was still no William. "I slackened my pace as I came
near home," she said, "fearing to hear that he was not come.
I listened until after one o'clock to every barking dog, cock-
fighting and other sports, but by Saturday, things were better.
I heard a foot go to the front of the house, turned around and
opened the gate. It was William!"

William had been gone for more than three weeks. He returned on June 7, and that night he and Dorothy stayed up until four o'clock in the morning, talking endlessly. There was much to talk about. John had returned to captain his ship; William's and Coleridge's book *Lyrical Ballads,* which had not gotten very good reviews, was about to be reprinted in a new edition; and, as always, he needed money. He had written some fifteen poems in Germany, and he was eager to have them printed.

He was eager, too, to have Coleridge join them at the Lakes. Then they could talk endlessly about poetry and literature. Coleridge must come. He must see the woods in yellow bloom; he must fish for pike in the lake; he could help William make pea sticks for the garden. He must indeed come to the Lakes, where, as Dorothy wrote in her journal, "it calls home the heart to quietness."

At the same time they must invite another writer who had grown increasingly dear to their lives, the gentle Charles Lamb.

❧ XV ❧

Gentle Charles Lamb

Knowledge and wisdom, gained from converse sweet
With books, or while he ranged the crowded streets
With a keen eye, and overflowing heart:
So genius triumphed over seeming wrong,
And poured out truth in works by thoughtful love
Inspired—works potent over smiles and tears.
And as round mountain-tops the lightning plays,
Thus innocently sported, breaking forth
As from a cloud of some grave sympathy,
Humour and wild instinctive wit, and all
The vivid flashes of his spoken words.

Written after the death of Charles Lamb
by: William Wordsworth

William and Dorothy felt they were living the best of all possible lives. Surely everyone longed for the lakes. How could Charles Lamb be content in London? Come, they wrote him, come.

Charles, however, did not hunger after country living. Indeed, to him even a short visit to the country soon grew tedious. He was distinctly a city boy. Charles had been born a Cockney in 1775; he would remain one all his life. Fortunately, he was blessed with a glorious sense of humor, because his life seemed to be one of continued tragedy. He was a man of medium height, about five feet six inches tall, but so fragile that on walks his friends used to pick him up in their arms and carry him across stone walls. He stammered, too, and was desperately poor. He had been unhappy in love; he worked at a job he disliked; he was subject to periods of depression; indeed, at one point he had a nervous breakdown for six weeks, "very agreeably in a mad house at Hoxton." He became the lifelong companion of his sister Mary, whom we remember today as the author of enchanting poetry and as co-author of that delightful introduction to Shakespeare, *Tales from Shakespeare*.

On September 26, 1796, Mary was spoken of in quite a different way. The *Morning Chronicle* presented the terrible story with stark simplicity: *One Lunatic Female* [Mary] *Had*

Killed Her Mother. It was only later that Charles wrote further details to Coleridge:

"My dearest friend—White or some of my friends or the public papers by this time may have informed you of the terrible calamities that have fallen on our family. I will only give you the outlines. My poor dear dearest sister in a fit of insanity has been the death of her own mother. I was at hand only time enough to snatch the knife out of her grasp. She is at present in a mad house, from whence I fear she must be moved to an hospital. God has preserved to me my senses— I eat and drink and sleep, and have my judgment I believe very sound. My poor father was slightly wounded, and I am left to take care of him and my aunt. Mr. Norris of the Blue-coat school has been very kind to us, and we have no other friend, but thank God I am very calm and composed, and able to do the best that remains to do. Write—as religious a letter as possible—but no mention of what is gone and done with—with me the former things are passed away, and I have something more to do that [than] to feel—

"God almighty

        Have us all in

        his keeping—

                    C. Lamb.

"Mention nothing of poetry. I have destroyed every vestige of past vanities of that kind. Do as you please, but if you publish, publish mine (I give free leave) without name or initial, and never send me a book, I charge you, you [your] own judgment will convince you not to take any notice of this yet to your dear wife.—You look after your family—I have my reason and strength left to take care of mine. I charge you don't think of coming to see me. Write. I will not see you if you come. God almighty love you and all of us—"

This shadow, the fact that Mary had killed her mother, together with her recurring insanity, haunted both her life and her brother's; indeed, it haunted even the lives of their friends.

One friend, Bryan Proctor, said, "Whenever the approach of one of her fits of insanity was announced by some irritability or change of manner, Lamb would take her under his arm to Hoxton Asylum. It was very affecting to encounter the young brother and his sister walking together on this painful errand. Mary herself, although sad, was very conscious of the necessity for the temporary separation from her only friend. They used to carry a straight jacket with them."

Mary used to worry about how her depression would affect her friends and wrote in such a vein to many of them: "Do not say anything, when you write, of our low spirits—it will vex Charles. You would laugh or you would cry, perhaps both, to see us sit together, looking at each other with long and rueful faces and saying how do you do and then we fall a-crying and say we will be better on the morrow."

Despite his private anguish, Lamb was a delightful friend. He could take the most serious subject and turn it into something joyful. He could take the most serious of persons— Wordsworth, for example, when he grew old and famous —and refer to him as, "you rascally old poet." The Lambs knew everyone: the Wordsworths, Robert Southey, William Godwin, Leigh Hunt, Tom Hood, William Hazlitt, even John Keats. Some of the literary lights, Charles disliked: Shelley and Byron, for example; but there was an "Archangel," a little damaged, whom he adored, a boy he had known in school. He was, of course, Samuel Taylor Coleridge. When Coleridge returned from Germany, he lived with Charles and Mary in their tiny flat where they all played host to literary London.

CHARLES LAMB

It was always to Lamb that Wordsworth wrote when he wanted advice on the copyediting of his manuscripts, or when he needed new books. Lamb was always in such severe financial straits that he could not buy the books Wordsworth requested unless he received money in advance, but he was an excellent critic and gave Wordsworth all sorts of advice and information about the literature of the day.

Friendship was extremely important to the writers of that period; they fed upon one another's ideas and excitement. When Coleridge and Wordsworth, or Coleridge and Lamb, were separated, there was real anguish in their letters. "Are we never to meet again. . . ." Lamb writes to Coleridge, "I have never met with anyone, never shall meet with anyone, who could or can compensate me for the loss of your society —I have no one to talk all these matters about to [*sic*]—I lack friends, I lack books to supply their absence."

Sometimes they quarreled. Before Coleridge and the Wordsworths left for Germany, Coleridge and Lamb had quarreled. The hurt feelings lingered; but on the return of the three travelers from Germany, the old friendships were reaffirmed.

When the Wordsworths wrote Charles, insisting he visit Cumberland, he replied, "With you and your Sister I could gang any where." But the truth was he did not long for Cumberland; he loved London too strongly. "I don't much care," he said, "if I never see a mountain in my life." No, that was not the world he wanted. Rather, he loved the lighted shops of the Strand and Fleet Street, the coaches and the wagons on the road, the bustle and wickedness around Covent Garden. It was "life awake if you awake at all hours of the night." It was the impossibility of being bored. Most people try to get away from the crowds, the dirt, and the noise but for Lamb it meant life. It was also the picturesque quality of the city that attracted him: the sun shining upon the houses and pavements; the old print shops; the bookstalls; the coffee houses with the steam of soup filtering from the kitchen; a pantomime show. London itself was a pantomime, he said— and a masquerade. It fed him, nourished him, and fully satisfied him.

"The wonder of these sights impels me into nightwalks about her crowded streets," he wrote of London. "And I often shed tears in the motley Strand from fulness of joy at so much Life." If these emotions were strange to Wordsworth, "so are your rural emotions to me," wrote Lamb. "No," he insisted, "my attachments are local, truly local. I have no passion for groves and valleys." And his mistresses, who were they? They were the old chairs and the old tables, the streets and squares he had known since his childhood.

Charles Lamb loved and admired the *Lyrical Ballads.* He thought Wordsworth one of the most exciting experimental- ists of his time. We know now that William was the first to embrace a concept of poetry that is, even today, vitally alive. There was not, Wordsworth insisted in the Preface to the second edition of *Lyrical Ballads,* any real difference between the language of prose and the language of poetry. His was the first publicly announced effort to write poems using everyday speech: sometimes the simple rural speech of northern Eng- land, sometimes the eloquent language of passion itself.

It had been a long time since English poetry had common feelings put into straightforward words. "Strange fits of pas- sion I have known," Wordsworth wrote, and he did seem to know the pain of passionate experience. He knew that poetry had to penetrate, that it had to deal with a "sort of half con- sciousness." He was in wholesale retreat from the "unfeeling language of the previous century." Much like our young peo- ple today, he wanted to "feel again." The poet, he insisted, has to clear and often to shape his own road; but he always emphasized the fact that emotions were complex and that language had to constantly fluctuate in order to express them accurately.

Wordsworth's ideas spread; Lamb helped scatter them to the London audience. It was good for William and Dorothy to have such a friend. "I am determined," said Charles, "to take what snatches of pleasure I can between the acts of our distressful drama." Promoting William's poetry was a pleasure that allowed him, temporarily, to forget his sister's instability.

Meanwhile, another drama was brewing among this circle of friends. Poor Coleridge, once so productive, had almost lost his gift for writing poetry. His ideas about life were as grandiose as ever, aided and exaggerated by the opium that he was now taking regularly, but friendships and poetry began to erode.

❧ XVI ❧

A Time of Friends

It was an April morning: fresh and clear
The Rivulet, delighting in its strength,
Ran with a young man's speed; and yet the voice
Of waters which the winter had supplied
Was softened down into a vernal tone.
The spirit of enjoyment and desire,
And hopes and wishes, from all living things
Went circling, like a multitude of sounds.

from: Poems on the Naming of Places
by: William Wordsworth

It had been a wretchedly cold winter; now it was the warm, muggy summer of 1800. For days, Dorothy and William had been expecting Coleridge; they had tried to find him lodgings, and they awaited his arrival impatiently. This time he would come with his wife Sara and his small son Hartley, to whom he was so devoted. His relationship with his wife was deteriorating. When she had desperately needed him, he had left her alone, and although she tried to be patient, she rarely understood the creative misery that wracked him like an illness.

When Dorothy finally saw Coleridge on that warm, June day, she thought he looked ill. They must have a picnic. They would sail on the lake at the foot of the mountain; they would have their tea on an island in the middle of the lake. Coleridge immediately felt better. In a valley, he said, he felt reposeful, but when he saw a mountain, his spirit wanted to soar with exhilaration.

They picnicked on a small island. Their kettle, steaming away with the promise of a good cup of tea, hung from a fir tree. The fire was made from fire apples (we would call them fir cones), and its smoke, floating upward, seemed as lazy as the group of friends. Later, they built a bigger fire and, as evening came, its light was reflected not only on their faces, but on the lake itself.

The Coleridges had taken advantage of an offer to lease a house, with ten rooms and a study, in Keswick, some thirteen mountainous miles from where the Wordsworths lived. They would stay a month with the Wordsworths, in Grasmere, and then move into their "small mansion," called Greta Hall. The Coleridges had barely moved to their own home when Samuel caught a deep cold, which was further complicated by the opium he was taking for relief. His ideas became grandiose: he would begin to translate enormous books and write philosophical works; he even attempted to write the life of Lessing, a task that had haunted him since his days in Germany.

Despite the thirteen miles between them, the Wordsworths frequently went to visit Coleridge; and he, when he could, came to see them at Grasmere. There, they would swim and sail on the lake. He was overjoyed with the excitement of the Lakes, but it was a different kind of enjoyment from that which Dorothy and William shared, deeply rooted in their own past; Coleridge's was the excitement of a boy on vacation. When he was well enough he would jump from rock to rock, never following the road down the mountain, making his own paths, beating back the bushes, stumbling, falling, tripping, leaping, only to arrive thoroughly exhausted at the bottom.

Every rock, every path, every tree, every grove seemed to have some significance to the people in the countryside, and William himself, during that year, wrote the long, beautiful "Poems on the Naming of Places." He explained that in the rural world feelings were often associated with a mountain or a rock named for either some piece of folklore or in honor of a real incident. There was, for example, "John's Grove," named for John Wordsworth, who loved the spot better than any other. There, a single beech tree grew within a grove of firs—a quiet place, a place with simply a thrush's nest, a few sheep, and the rocks that had been the playground of the Wordsworths' youth. And here were trees that became "Mary's Beeches" after Wordsworth had walked "far among the ancient trees" with the woman he was to marry.

For Coleridge, the countryside had a different meaning, compounded partly of a deep peace (a quality that seemed to be eluding him more and more as he grew older), partly of his affection for William (answering the constant need for some supportive friend), and partly of just great exuberance. "I never find myself alone within the embracement of rocks and hills," he said, "but my spirit careens, driving and eddying like a leaf in Autumn; a wild activity of thoughts, imaginations, feelings and impulses, emotion arises up from within me; a sort of bottom wind that blows to no point of a compass comes from where I know not whence but agitates the whole of me; my whole being is filled with waves that roll and tumble. . . . I think my soul must have pre-existed in the body of a chamois chaser."

Then he would grow ill again, and the Wordsworths had to visit him. Dorothy did so often, starting off in the late afternoon and arriving frequently as late as eleven o'clock at night. Despite the fact that the guest helped with the housework, Sara Coleridge was bitter—and jealous, too. These friends of her husband's had taken him away from her before, and she always feared they would do so again. Once, Dorothy stayed with them a week; she and Samuel walked and gathered raspberries, talked, and generally made Sara unhappy.

Dorothy and Coleridge were fascinated by the activities of young Hartley. They would watch him scolding flowers while they talked of many things, even ghosts. Coleridge said he had actually seen ghosts and, always haunted by the supernatural, he began work on his great poem "Christabel." In October of that year, Coleridge walked to Grasmere, bringing with him the second part of the poem. He was again lonely; the little attention his wife had given him had been transferred to their newly born son, Derwent.

Coleridge was growing depressed more frequently, and the comfort of the Wordsworths' companionship was meaningful and important to him. Dorothy had few complaints, only that the house was too near the road, and a bit too small. Because of its location, if Coleridge were sick it would not be quiet enough.

It had been a glorious summer: their brother John had come for a long stay, Coleridge was near, Mary Hutchinson visited at length. Now that Sara had to care for a new child, Hartley Coleridge stayed with Dorothy. ". . . he is a sweet companion," she wrote Jane, "always alive and of a delightful temper. I shall find it very difficult to part with him when we have once got him here."

She was busy, too, at that time, reading German in the hope of eventually being able to translate, but mostly she was writing out her brother's poems, baking, cooking, and always talking and walking.

When necessary, she nursed not only her brother, who always had an adverse physical reaction to writing poetry, but Coleridge too, who had an incredible set of problems among which were boils and arthritis, nervousness, depression, bloodshot eyes, and, finally, rheumatic fever. Dorothy complained that Sara was "a bad nurse for Coleridge, but she has several great merits. She is much, very much, to be pitied, for when one party is ill matched, the other necessarily must be so too. She would have made a very good wife to many another man, but for Coleridge!! . . . She is an excellent nurse to her suckling children (I mean to the best of her skill, for she employs her time often foolishly enough about them). Derwent is a sweet lovely Fatty—she suckles him entirely—he has no other food. She is sure to be a sad fiddle faddler. From about ½ past 10 on Sunday morning till two she did nothing but wash and dress her 2 children and herself, and was just ready for dinner."

Perhaps poor Sara was simply retreating from a world that was too difficult for her. It was obvious now, although Dorothy refused to see it, that Coleridge was resorting to far too much laudanum and, instead of racing up mountains, was racing down them into an abyss from which nothing could rescue him.

Coleridge commuted back and forth to London, trying to make money by working on the *Morning Post.* The Lake Country was too damp for him, and he liked the excitement of London where he could talk to Charles Lamb and William Godwin; yet he longed, too, for rural peace and the comfort given him by the one woman he was to love perhaps more than any other—Sara Hutchinson, the sister of Mary Hutchinson, Wordsworth's future wife.

Coleridge visited the Hutchinsons whenever he could, enraging his own Sara and growing ever more guilty and depressed. Yet the Wordsworth and Coleridge families became increasingly involved with the Hutchinsons. As for Coleridge's love for his wife, all the nagging in the world, he said, did not change the fact that she was the mother of his children, and even if he had to remove himself physically, he would never truly leave her.

Finally, in the spring of 1802, William and Mary made plans to be married the following October. After this decision, brother and sister became inseparable. He wrote poems to her and felt his only rest was to fall asleep against her shoulder. He grew dependent on her eyes and ears for some of the evocations of his own poetry. That spring, Dorothy wrote in her journal that they had seen "a few daffodils close to the waterside; we fancied that the lake had floated the weeds ashore, and that the little colony had so sprung up. But as we went along, there were more and yet more; and at last, under the boughs of the trees, we saw that there was a long belt of them along the shore, about the breadth of a country turnpike road. I never saw daffodils so beautiful; they grew among the stones that bulged about them. Some rested their heads on these stones as on a painful weariness, and the rest tossed and reeled and danced and seemed as if they verily laughed with the wind that blew them over the lake; and they looked so gay, ever glancing, ever changing. The wind blew directly over the lake to them."

These are the images that William incorporated into his poem that captured "a host of golden daffodils," proving that although Mary might become his wife, Dorothy was still to be his muse.

ROAD TO KESWICK

❧ XVII ❧

Marriage

The spot was made by Nature for herself;
The travellers know it not, and 'twill remain
Unknown to them; but it is beautiful;
And if a man should plant his cottage near,
Should sleep beneath the shelter of its trees,
And blend its waters with his daily meal,
He would so love it, that in his death-hour
Its image would survive among his thoughts:
And therefore, my sweet Mary, this still Nook,
With all its beeches, we have named from You!

from: To M. H. (Mary Hutchinson)
by: William Wordsworth

"It is a beautious evening, calm and free; the holy time is quiet as a nun." So begins one of Wordsworth's most famous sonnets and one of the few pieces of writing in which he talked about his daughter Caroline, the child of Annette. "Dear child, dear girl, thou walkest with me here."

They walked together along the seashore of Calais, in France, one night following a very hot day, and as they walked along the pier Wordsworth started his poem. It was more than the setting sun ("the broad sun is sinking down in its tranquility;") that he saw go down that night, it was as though night had fallen on his first passionate love, and a new world was to emerge on the morrow.

Life had changed. It now seemed possible that Wordsworth would have a little money: the family estate would soon be settled, and the old Earl of Lonsdale's son would pay the debt that had so long haunted William. Now he could get married.

The period from 1797 to 1802 had been extraordinary for Wordsworth. He had written, with feverish intensity, some of his greatest poems. In a sudden burst of creative energy, they had come pouring from him—the words, the feelings—and he had caught them like butterflies using them in his writings. It was as though a new time was starting for him, a time as ripe as spring—verdant in poetry and people. Wordsworth's world had opened up. In Dorothy's journal on May 16, 1802, appear the names of those who meant so much to him:

S. T. Coleridge.

Dorothy Wordsworth.   William Wordsworth.

Mary Hutchinson.   Sara Hutchinson.

William.   Coleridge.   Mary.

Dorothy.   Sara.

16th May

1802

John Wordsworth.

They were all extraordinarily close, and not only in the pages of the journal. There was, on the way to Keswick, a rock called "Sara's rock," and there William and Mary (his wife to be), Dorothy, their brother John, Coleridge and his love Sara Hutchinson, for whom the rock was named (and who sustained him, as Mary was to sustain William), carved their names in friendship and love.

Dorothy, William, and Coleridge were the "wild ones," who needed the sustaining influence of others: the quiet love of Mary for William and, for Dorothy, too; the sustaining affection of Sara Hutchinson for Coleridge. Sara Coleridge, for her part, although she knew of the other Sara's existence, was never to be as jealous of her as she was of the Wordsworths—they who loved each other with a terrible intensity, who walked forever in the night, who did not care what other people thought, who often arrived as the moon came over the cottage, who departed who knew when?

Yes, the wild ones needed those who were less wild. Coleridge, who loved Mary as well as Sara Hutchinson, knew a depth of happiness with those two sisters, and with William and Dorothy—a brief happiness—that he was never to feel again. For William, happiness would be lifelong as Mary Hutchinson gave him the stability and affection he needed. She would give him a comforting caress; she would put his feet not on high mountains and crags but on the ground, where he could gain a new strength. He would continue to roam and compose poetry with Dorothy, but with Mary he would be an admirable husband.

There had been, of course, another time of wildness for William: the time of Annette. But as he thought about his forthcoming marriage to Mary Hutchinson, he knew he must tell Annette of his plan. He must make some kind of financial provision for his daughter Caroline; he must take a last look at his old life.

First, Dorothy and William went to the Hutchinson farm to tell Mary of William's intention to make the journey to France. Dorothy, loving Mary as she did, still felt an anguish she could not explain as they took leave of Dove Cottage, even though they would eventually return to live there. She turned to her journal, writing simply at first: "William is eating his broth," and then she added, "I must prepare to go; the swallows I must leave them, the well, the gardens, the roses, all, dear creatures!! They sang last night after I was in bed, seemed to be singing to one another just before they settled to rest for the night. Well, I must go, Farewell." And the farewell was really an adieu to her total involvement with her brother.

The Wordsworths and Coleridge, who had joined them, began to walk. The melancholy they felt was almost tangible. They went slowly, thinking of their deep love for one another, observing and commenting on the world around them. They walked through hills, where brushes sang and cattle fed among green-brown hillocks, and ruins sprang into view.

They spent about ten days with Mary, and then William and Dorothy went on to London. By the end of July, they were ready to proceed to Dover, to the packet that would take them to Calais, which at that time was a resort town. There was nothing to do in Calais, but one could walk forever on its sandy beaches. One could also swim from the pier, and one could, of course, write poetry.

Wordsworth wrote seven sonnets while he was in Calais, all linked to his dual feelings about France and England: France, the country that had given him his first love; England, the country to which he had given his heart. William had become impassioned in France before, and now he "took fire" again. This time, his thoughts were not connected so much with Annette, as they had been previously, but were concerned with the changes that had taken place in his own feelings. Once he had loved not only Annette but also France and the spirit of revolution. Then, with Bonaparte—and dictatorship, Wordsworth's dreams had disappeared.

Between Annette and William there was now nothing except their child. Annette, however, had pride in the poet and their daughter, but the personal feelings she and William once had for each other were dissipated. In one thing they agreed: they hated Napoleon Bonaparte, the man who had spoiled their dream for France. To each he symbolized something different. For Wordsworth, Napoleon symbolized tyranny and the death of the Republican dream. Annette's dislike was more immediate: Napoleon had done nothing for Royalist hopes. He who could have restored her heroes, the Bourbon Kings of France, had done nothing but proclaim himself an emperor. Where once England and France had united, as Annette and Wordsworth had united as lovers, now they were enemies. Only for a short time, between March, 1802, and

133

May, 1803, had there been peace between the two countries, brought about by the peace treaty of Amiens. It was this treaty that made the Wordsworths' visit possible.

Now, as William walked along the seashore with his daughter, he realized that the ten years between 1792 and 1802 made an enormous difference. As a matter of fact, now he could barely speak French. At one point he had been fluent; now the language came tightly to his tongue, and Caroline knew no English. Yet there seemed to be a bond between them. She was a dear little girl.

Those ten years had changed Annette. For her there had not been the calm and peace of Grasmere and Alfoxden. For her there had been the daily intrigue and danger of life in the underground. During those years she had known nothing but a commanding desire to help the Royalist movement. Her brother had nearly been killed during the Terror, and she and her sister were known to the government as supporters of the refugees who would not take the new oath of allegiance to Bonaparte. Annette was called Widow Williams. Her house could at any time be searched; friends could at any time be arrested. Years later, when the Bourbons were restored to the throne, she was given a small pension, but during all those lonely years there was nothing but the fear of a knock on the door—the fear of tyranny. She had lived a life different from William's, and there was little chance for a lasting marriage between them. Both knew it now, and it was with relief that Dorothy and William returned to Dover, in England. There, on the twenty-ninth of August, 1802, they sat upon the Dover cliffs and "looked upon France with many a melancholy and tender thought." Annette and William would continue to be friends, and they would meet once again eighteen years later. But now it was Mary to whom William gave his thoughts.

On October 4, they were married at Brompton Church, located near the Hutchinson farm at Scarborough.

Dorothy was so overwrought that she could not attend the wedding ceremony, and it was sweet Sara Hutchinson who prepared the wedding breakfast.

There were no wedding presents, only a new dress for Mary from John Wordsworth. On their wedding journey back to Grasmere they had wedding presents enough. They had sunshine and showers, plus good talk, love, and cheerfulness—and the company of Dorothy.

❧ *XVIII* ❧

A Changing Scene

"What, you are stepping westward?"—"Yea"
—'Twould be a wildish destiny,
If we, who thus together roam
In a strange Land, and far from home,
Were in this place the guests of Chance:
Yet who would stop, or fear to advance,
Though home or shelter he had none,
With such a sky to lead him on?

from: Stepping Westward
by: William Wordsworth

"Again I have neglected to write my Journal, New Year's Day is passed, Old Christmas day and I have recorded nothing. It is today *Tuesday,* January 11th."

Dorothy's journal, which had once recorded in great detail all her daily activities, now barely drew her interest. It was 1803, a year of many changes for the Wordsworths both within their home and within their country, which, in the course of the year, would be frightened by the fear of a possible invasion from France.

The daily cares were to increase, delightful cares for Dorothy that made the journal no longer so important. Perhaps, too, she felt she was no longer important to William. Although she continued to write many letters, we do not know what her intimate thoughts were from this point on; the immediacy and creative beauty of her journal disappeared. The last few entries do not record lines of poetry. They are, instead, little domestic notes: "We ate some potted beef on horseback and sweet cake," she would explain; "we ate gingerbread; the weather was intensely cold."

During this early January of 1803 the weather fluctuated unbelievably. One day was mild as spring, with beautiful evenings and quiet nights; the next morning arrived with fierce winds and dreadful cold. It was so frigid that the whole household stayed in bed as long as it could—Mary gratefully because she was pregnant. Her child would be born in July.

Coleridge came over on January 11. His health was very poor, and he talked interminably of a trip to some land that would bring warmth back into his body, perhaps the Canary Islands.

He was now miserable, not only because of his health, but because his marriage had almost disintegrated. Like many writers, Coleridge had little patience with those who did not share his creative life, and that was particularly true in his relation to his wife Sara. There was no doubt that Mrs. Coleridge was a difficult woman; but she had just had a new baby and was, herself, tense and unhappy. Coleridge threatened her sense of security by constantly going to the Wordsworth's and, even more, by saying that he must leave; that his health was such that he must have months of tranquility. He was always annoyed by his wife's attacks on the Wordsworths and in one letter chastised her cruelly:

"It is without any feeling of Pride in myself, to say—that . . . in the quantity and quality of natural endowments, whether of Feeling, or of Intellect, you are the inferior. Therefore it would be preposterous to expect that I should see with your eyes, and dismiss my Friends from *my* heart, . . . but it is not preposterous, in me, on the contrary I have a *right* to expect and demand, that you should to a certain degree love and act kindly to those whom I deem worthy of my Love.—If you read this Letter and half the Tenderness with which it is written, it will do you and both of us good."

Although Coleridge would demand over and over again that Sara love those he loved, she could not do it. Their worlds were far too different. Hers, one of domestication; his, one of wild fancy, a world becoming blurred and even muddied by the opium he was still taking regularly. The drug not only deteriorated his mind, but it increased his susceptibility to illness. Now, following a long walk to Grasmere, he would often become ill. Once he had enjoyed walking when the weather was fierce; now, when he walked through the rain, "like splinters of flint," he suffered from exposure.

He experienced, too, the terrible depression of a poet who knows his genius is disappearing and knows, as well, that his own continual use of drugs is partially responsible. He promised himself he would take no more. "I took no opium or laudanum," he said, writing in pride to his friend Tom Wedgwood. Immediately, however, he confessed, "but at 8 o'clock, unable to bear the stomach uneasiness and . . . the aching of my Limbs, I took two large Tea spoonfuls of Ether in a wine glass of Camphorated Gum water and a third Tea spoonful at ten o'clock—I received complete relief, my body calmed, my sleep placid; but when I awoke in the morning, my right hand, with three of the Fingers, was swollen and inflamed."

Among many artists of the period, the idea was common that opium could in some way inspire their work, instead of eventually destroying it. Coleridge was looking for a world he could not have: a world of peace, a world that, at the very best, is a dream. So more and more he relied upon drugs. He tried bang, a kind of Indian hemp, and hensbane. Nothing, however, helped and, sadly, he admitted his poetic demise: "The poet is dead in me," he wrote; "I was once a volume of gold leaf, rising and riding on every blessed fancy, but I have beaten myself back into weight and density, and now I sink in quicksilver. I have *forgotten* how to make a rhyme." Yes, Coleridge's world was changing; his relations to other people were changing too. The high point of his poetic career was over, even the high point of his great genius for being a friend.

Changes, too, were occurring for William and Dorothy. Now that they had a little money they wondered if they should risk investing it. John, whom they loved dearly, was about to take a trip to the East. He had asked his brother and sister to invest a good portion of their inheritance in the voyage. Could they safely do so? Dorothy, William, and John left it to their brother Richard to handle the financial matters. Dorothy wrote intimately:

"My Dear John,

"Richard has informed me that you are [gone] down to Gravesend, to return no more from your ship. God send a blessing on you and your whole voyage and bring you back to us again in health and prosperity!"

She longed to give her brother the money for the voyage, but felt she could not. To her letter she added sweetly that even their old housekeeper said, "if I could but see Maister John I would send all the money that ever I have for a venture with him!" But the poor old soul, said Dorothy, had nothing. On May 6, 1803, *The Earl of Abergavenny*, John's ship, sailed for the East.

That spring was unseasonable, first cold and dry, then intensely hot. Yet, by June, Dorothy thought the spot they lived in the most beautiful in the world "with the sky enclosing it so that there seemed no other place beyond, and it seemed as beautiful a place as there need be in a beautiful world." Although Coleridge visited them less, he wrote that he was in good health. Dorothy rejoiced. Once again she and William walked together. They would wait for the rain to stop, then walk on the most fertile of earth. "The softest green covers the mountains even to the very top," Dorothy reported. They decided a trip would be ideal, and one with Coleridge the best possible. Coleridge's doctor had prescribed a change of scene for him and a tour would do him good. Why not a trip to Scotland?

Just a few short weeks after Mary and William's baby was born—a son named John—William and Dorothy left mother and child in the care of Sara Hutchinson and undertook their journey.

First, they must have a horse—a stout one, no matter how old—and a jaunting cart in which they could ride in the back, with a place in the middle for the few bags they would take, and a box for the driver to sit upon. Coleridge, like a child, wrote, "it has all sorts of conveniences," but it was to be a remarkably inconvenient form of traveling, particularly for Coleridge who was overly susceptible to the cold, wet summer of Scotland.

Scotland always had a romantic meaning to the Wordsworths. From nearly every place they lived, they had been able to stare across the River Solway and see beyond the distant mountains that formed the Scottish border. Scotland was, of course, the land of Robert Burns, who had been one of Wordsworth's greatest inspirations. As the three friends set out on that August morning, they made a strange group:

> *Their exterior semblance did belie*
> *Their soul's immensity.*

Indeed, from the records we have, their "exterior semblance" was a little strange. Coleridge, in soiled trousers and a blue jacket with brass buttons (which he often wore when preaching in Unitarian pulpits), was barely able to button the coat around his portly stomach. No longer was he the handsome young poet he once had been. Wordsworth, never remarkably handsome, wore a dirty brown suit and a wide straw hat to protect his eyes. Dorothy never cared what she wore on such trips. What did it matter when you were in a jaunting cart?

As they moved through the countryside, some thought them gypsies. Coleridge would try to sleep in the carriage, depressed and cold most of the way, and generally disgruntled. Despite William's and Dorothy's extraordinary sensitivities and gifts for observation, they were poor travelers. Germany had disappointed them. Scotland did too, until they got to the Highlands. Even Burns's house was a disappointment: it was greatly neglected now that the Burnses were all dead. It was dirty, with only a few pathetic plants in the window. Dorothy was shocked that no stone marked the spot of Burns's grave. Both she and William could not help but wonder how a man of Burns's sensitivity could have lived in such "unpoetic ground." In contrast to their beautiful dales, the area around Dumfries, Burns's home, was barren. The gorse in bloom had already withered and died. "Surely Scotland should replant their forests," said Dorothy, ever the conservationist; although "The ground all over heaves and swells like a sea . . . there are neither trees nor hedgerows. . . ." The Scottish inns were inferior to those of England. Their parlors were dirty; tea came late. Yet Dorothy was impressed that even the miners had small libraries.

Most days were rainy, but when the weather was good they rode along joyously. "I can always walk over a moor with a light foot," Dorothy said. "I seem to be drawn more closely to nature in such places than anywhere else; or rather I feel more strongly the power of nature over me, and am better satisfied with myself for being able to find enjoyment in what unfortunately to many persons is either dismal or insipid."

Not infrequently, Coleridge was ill and had to stay in whatever cottage he could find, while William and Dorothy tramped off by themselves, coming upon waterfalls, looking at cottages and little huts that reminded Dorothy of prints from Captain Cook's voyages, discovering some brook or small river. "The beauties of a brook or river must be sought," she said, "and the pleasure is going in search of them. Those of a lake or of the sea come to you of themselves." They were delighted by the moss-covered houses that were called "fog houses."

Coleridge, aware of the extent of his illness, said later: "I soon found I was a burden to them, and Wordsworth, himself a brooder over his painful hypochondriacal sensations, was not my fittest companion."

William found Coleridge "in bad spirits and somewhat too much in love with his own dejection."

They parted, and Coleridge, "happy alone," walked madly by himself, and was even arrested once as a spy. William and Dorothy went on to visit Walter Scott, the famous novelist. "His local attachments," Dorothy said, "are more strong than those of any person I ever saw, his whole heart and soul seem to be devoted to the Scottish Streams, Yarrow and Tweed, Tiviot and the rest of them, of which we hear in the Border Ballads, and I am sure that there is not a story ever told by the firesides in that neighborhood that he cannot repeat. . . . He is a man of very sweet manners, mild, cordial and cheerful."

They returned to Grasmere in September, 1803, to find the countryside deeply worried by the fear of a French invasion. William joined the Grasmere Volunteers. "We turned out almost to a man," he said; but his real contribution to the English effort was in the patriotic sonnets he composed that year. He worked, too, on a handful of poems inspired by his Scottish trip, while Dorothy sat beside him composing, in reflection, a journal of the tour.

The feared invasion did not come and life grew quiet again.

Even Coleridge offered no distraction; he had sailed for Malta, to be gone three years. He was not, however, out of their thoughts. How could he be? William was busily at work on a long poem to Coleridge, a poem that would become *The Prelude,* the great adventure into "the making of a poet's mind" that Wordsworth would continue for the rest of his life.

❧ *XIX* ❧

They that go down to the sea in ships

The Sheep-boy whistled loud, and lo!
That instant, startled by the shock,
The Buzzard mounted from the rock
Deliberate and slow:
Lord of the air, he took his flight;
Oh! could he on that woeful night
Have lent his wing, my Brother dear,
For one poor moment's space to Thee,
And all who struggled with the Sea,
When safety was so near.

from: Elegiac Verses
In Memory of My Brother,
John Wordsworth
by: William Wordsworth

"Come," wrote William to his brother John, "if only for a fortnight; we long to see you." John, who had just returned from his voyage on *The Earl of Abergavenny,* was now planning another trip. His last two had not been very successful. The first—the one in which William and Dorothy wisely had decided not to invest—had been a financial failure. During the second trip the trading had picked up, and John had made a small profit. He was now in London, reluctant to go to the Lakes he adored because he wanted to use the time to make his third voyage a major success. Then he might move to the Lakes permanently with his sister and brother and dear Coleridge—if Coleridge should ever come back from his eternal traveling.

John led a more adventurous life than William or Dorothy, and they were fascinated by his tales of distant lands, which were as exciting as the *Arabian Nights* stories that had so fascinated William as a boy. Now John was not only a captain, but a hero. On his last voyage, the ship he manned had been in a convoy that encountered a French squadron near the Straits of Malacca. With the help of the *Abergavenny* the French had been forced to retreat, and on John's return to England he had received five hundred guineas from the directors of the East India Company, under whose authority he sailed.

Now everything looked promising. In the first place, through his Uncle, William Cookson, the great abolitionist, John had met another abolitionist, more influential in the government: William Wilberforce. Through his help John was to receive one of the best trade routes in the East, the Bengal to China route. His cargo would, today, equal a million-dollars, and John himself speculated heavily on it. This time William invested a sum of money. *The Earl of Abergavenny* was a good ship, carrying some four hundred people: the ship's company numbered two hundred, and soldiers and passengers made up the other two hundred. All the passenger fares went directly to the Captain of any East Indiaman. John was eager to get started: "one must get safe and soon to Bengal," he wrote; "I mean before any other ship of the season; I have no doubt but that I shall make a good voyage of it, if not a very great one, at least this is the general opinion." He asked for more of William's poetry, as he had been particularly taken by "To a Butterfly," "The Cuckoo," and "The Leech Gatherer." He longed, too, to be with his brother and sister—but he had to go.

At the beginning of February, 1805, he put to sea. He did not get far. On February 5, a westerly gale hit the channel off Portland Bill, traditionally one of the hardest places to sail in the English Channel. It had been the horror and nemesis of sailors for years. Most boats avoided it completely, but the Indiamen usually ran the risk—sometimes too much of a risk —because their large size made them seem invulnerable.

Off Portland Bill there is a terrible race and floodtide. It extends sometimes for a mile, sometimes two, sometimes four. The seas in it are irregular. Because the channel narrows at this point between the promontories of both England and France, the tidal stream runs strongly. All of the headlands have submerged shelfs beneath them. On the sea bottom there is a wall of rock, sometimes as high as sixty feet, and the tide rages and bubbles above it. Sometimes the tidal current moves as rapidly as six knots; occasionally it joins with an inshore tidal stream, disturbing the water even more. The sea there has been described as a pot on the boil; waves come from all directions. Many sailors, having once attempted to run the Bill, never attempt it again; others have seen their ships actually flung over on their side.

John Wordsworth carried a pilot on board the *Abergavenny,* but as he began to cross one of these races the wind suddenly died away and a strong tide set the ship to westward. Suddenly, it drifted into the breakers, and the sea began to lash the ship. At five P.M., she struck a reef.

The night was dreadful. As the storm's fury rose, one tidal surge would throw the ship on the reef, another would toss her like driftwood into the raging breakers. With great seamanship, *The Earl of Abergavenny* was finally dislodged from the reef. But, waterlogged and clumsy, she could not sail into the nearest bay. There were ships now standing by, but the race was too strong for any to get near. Throughout it all, Captain Wordsworth stood on the "hencoop"; he knew his ship was going down. Suddenly, a great wave crashed, and he was washed overboard. He struggled gallantly, but uselessly, against the raging waves. Finally, the sea swallowed him. His efforts were to no advantage. "What," said William later, "could it avail in such a sea?" Not only did John drown, but three-quarters of the persons aboard the ship went down with her. *The Earl of Abergavenny* had foundered close to the spot where another East Indiaman had been wrecked in 1776.

Richard (William's other brother who was, at the time, living in London) was the first to receive the news of John's death. There were no telephones, of course, and he therefore wrote William. His letter was picked up by Mary's sister, Sara Hutchinson, who evidently read the news in a newspaper at the same time. She was disturbed and shaken, for there had been a gentle understanding that she and John might marry.

When Sara reached Dove Cottage, she was troubled to find that William and Mary were out walking; only Dorothy was in the house. Upon hearing the disastrous news, she immediately went into deep shock. On returning home, William did his best to comfort her. Only the day before, Dorothy had said, "John is in such great spirits." Now everything had changed.

William, writing to Richard, stated his feelings concisely: "The set [of their family] is now broken." Both Dorothy and Mary fell ill. William did his best to console everyone, but he could not get over his own grief. "John was very dear to me, and my heart will never forget him," he wrote. He asked for news of the tragedy—any kind of news.

Shortly thereafter, he wrote to Charles Lamb, who worked for the East India Company. Perhaps he could send news. There were rumors reaching them that perhaps poor seamanship on John's part had caused the accident, but the family wanted any kind of news they could get. Lamb wrote to reassure them that the authorities felt John had done his best.

Dorothy and William could not turn emotionally to Richard; he was entirely too phlegmatic. He was, Dorothy said, a "curious brother." Still, William tried to express some of his feelings in a letter to him. "God defend any body from suffering what we have suffered, and still do suffer. No words can express the love which we had of poor John, and the daily and perpetual pleasure which we had in looking forward to the time when he would be at liberty to settle among us. He loved every thing which we did, and every thing about us

151

here incessantly reminds us of him and our irreparable loss." Then he added, "But I will not distress you, for you can give us no relief."

Even William and Dorothy could give each other little relief. They wrote endless letters to friends: to the Beaumonts, wealthy, sensitive patrons of the arts; to Dorothy's ever faithful friend, Jane Pollard. Always the tone was the same. To Lady Beaumont she wrote, "Wherever we go we shall know what would have been John's sentiments and feelings if he had been at our side—for he was true and constant as the light of heaven—he seemed to have been made for the best sort of happiness which is to be found in this world for his whole delight was in peace and Love and the beautiful works of this fair creation . . . I cannot speak of him as he was; I must have done."

Only their walks and their children soothed them. Mary and William had a new daughter, Dorothy—called Dora— and her presence was their chief delight and consolation. For the rest, their days were consumed with anxiety. The house was getting too small; their walks were too melancholy; the very area was tinged with memories, and each recollection was a fresh sorrow. It seemed at times "Sunshine and darkness, starlight and moonlight, calm weather and fierce winds were all doleful."

They longed for Coleridge and talked about him incessantly. If only he were there to share their grief! Why did he not write?

Spring melted some of the hard shell of ice that seemed to have grown around their hearts. Friends helped. Charles and Mary Lamb in particular had been unusually kind; they who knew so much pain could share a deep, sympathetic understanding of tragedy with others.

Finally, Dorothy realized she had to shake off her melancholy. It did not matter that she always seemed to see before her the image of her brother John; she must remember there were children to look after, a life to be concerned with. Still, she said, "I can never again have a perfect—that is, an unchastised, joy in this world."

By early summer, things were better; she was rewriting her journal of the Scottish tour, though always with the thought that John would no longer read it, just as he would not read the poems William would write. "But the birds did rejoice in the rain," she said, and William was now returning to the life of fishing and writing "verses to the memory of our lost Brother," who had so loved to fish in the solitude of the mountains. Dorothy could hardly bear to go to those spots that John had loved. Twice she went near the lake that he enjoyed so much, only to break into tears.

Visitors came—visitors and friends, not Coleridge, still away, but others—the Clarksons, the Threlkelds. The Threlkelds, who were distant cousins of Dorothy's, noticed she had grown thin. Suddenly, she appeared much older. Her face was pained, sunken, and gaunt with grief.

Traveling on the continent, Coleridge had missed letters from his friends. Wordsworth knew Coleridge would be shocked. "I tremble," he said, "for the moment when he is to hear of my brother's death; it will distress him to the heart—and his poor body cannot bear sorrow. He loved my brother, and he knows how we at Grasmere loved him."

It was not until the very end of March that the news of the shipwreck reached Malta, where Coleridge was staying. A friend, Lady Ball, brought the story to him. He immediately broke down. "Your strong feelings are too great for your health," she said. "I hope you will soon recover your spirits." But to Coleridge John's death meant, as it did to Wordsworth, that "the set" had been broken, the set of friendship and family that had meant so much to him. He wrote in his notebook, ten days after he had received the news, "Oh dear John Wordsworth!" He tried to return to England, but he did not know how; the war had made it impossible.

For her part, Mary Lamb sent a poem to Dorothy:

> *Why is he wandering on the sea?*
> *Coleridge should now with Wordsworth be.*
> *By slow degrees, he'd steal away*
> *Their woe, and gently bring a ray*
> *(So happily he'd time relief)*
> *Of comfort from their very grief.*
> *He'd tell them that their brother dead*
> *When years have passed o'er their head,*
> *Will be remember'd with such holy,*
> *True, and perfect melancholy*
> *That ever this lost brother John*
> *Will be their heart's companion.*
> *His voice they'll always hear,*
> *His face they'll always see,*
> *There's naught in life so sweet*
> *As such a memory.*

In a few weeks the Lambs were to be overwhelmed in their own grief as Charles, once again, led Mary to the asylum.

William, too, tried to express his grief in poetry. It was not, however, until he went to John's favorite fishing spot that his memories overwhelmed him. "Poor William was overcome . . ." wrote Dorothy to Lady Beaumont, "and with floods of tears wrote those verses." They were not published until 1842. Wordsworth entitled them "Elegiac Verses in Memory of My Brother, John Wordsworth."

❧ XX ❧

The Opium Eater when young

Yet are they here the same unbroken knot
Of human Beings, in the self-same spot!
   Men, women, children, yea the frame
   Of the whole spectacle the same!
Only their fire seems bolder, yielding light,
Now deep and red, the colouring of night;
   That on their Gipsy-faces falls,
   Their bed of straw and blanket-walls.
—Twelve hours, twelve bounteous hours are gone,
      while I
Have been a traveller upon open sky,
   Much witnessing of change and cheer,
   Yet as I left I find them here!

from: Gipsies
by: William Wordsworth

"Her face was of Egyptian brown, rarely in a woman of English birth had I seen a more determined Gypsy turn. The eyes were not soft, nor were they fierce or bold; but they were wild and startling and hurried in their nature. Her manner was warm, even ardent, her sensibilities seemed constitutionally deep, and some subtle fire of impassioned intellect apparently burned within her, which was being alternately pushed forward into a conspicuous expression by the irresistible instincts of her temperament, and then immediately checked in obedience to the decorum of her sex and her age and her maidly condition (for she had rejected all offers of marriage out of pure sisterly regard to her brother and his children), gave to her whole demeanor and to her conversation an air of embarrassment, and even of self-conflict, that was sometimes distressing to witness."

This is the most vivid contemporary description we have of Dorothy Wordsworth; it was written by a young man, Thomas De Quincey, after his first visit with the Wordsworths. Years later, Thomas De Quincey would write under the name of "The Opium Eater."

One of the greatest essayists of his age, De Quincey left us many literary reminiscences of the Wordsworth group. He was one of those men who took a passionate interest in poetry and

the poets who created it. When he was just seventeen, still
a schoolboy, he had run across the small volume called
Lyrical Ballads containing Wordsworth's early poetry and
Coleridge's "The Ancient Mariner." His admiration for both
men was unbounded. Long before he met either, he had done
everything to make their writing well known because, curiously enough, he thought both Coleridge and Wordsworth,
particularly the latter, were not receiving the attention that
time would eventually give them. While at college, De Quincey spoke their names with such sympathy that he was, he
said, constantly rebuffed about his enthusiasm for such "mod-
erns." Each rebuttal only made him more eager to meet his
heroes: the two poets who had fought against the current
artificiality of language and had chosen instead a beautiful
simplicity that carried the reader back to nature, back to the
spirit and the soul from which all poetry is derived.

Thomas De Quincey had, like Coleridge and Wordsworth,
suffered a painful childhood. His father was a self-made man
who had not been to college, but who wanted to provide an
education for his sons, despite the fact that his own resources
were always sorely tried. Mrs. De Quincey was, for that day,
a rather extraordinary woman. She constantly redesigned and
remodeled every house she lived in, each time effecting great
improvement, yet tying up the De Quincey income in the
process.

Her son, Thomas, had been born on August 15, 1785. In
the ten years that followed, death was his frequent companion: first his sister Jane died when he was but five years old;
a year later his sister Elizabeth died; two years later his father
died, and he soon found himself alienated from his mother.
He said later that even as a small boy he had "heard the
sound of a wind that might have swept the fields of immortal-

ity for a thousand centuries. Many times, since, upon summer days, when the sun is about the hottest, I have remarked
that the same wind arising and uttering the same hollow,
solemn Memnoian but saintly swell: It is in this world one
great audible symbol of eternity."

It was no wonder that life seemed difficult to cope with
satisfactorily. Always frail, Thomas was frequently subject to
illness. Always solitary, he could not adjust to his brother,
older and stronger, "horrid and pugilistic." At school he was
always unhappy. Miserable at Oxford, he began to wander
around the countryside. Once, in London, a usurer allowed
him to sleep in one of his unfurnished rooms; a girl of ten
years old lived in an adjoining room. The child and the boy
slept on cold floors and wandered around London together.
Thomas saw the seamy side of the world before he saw its
beauty, and at times he had only the small volume of *Lyrical
Ballads* to comfort him. Finally, he and his mother became
reconciled, and shortly thereafter, just before William, Dorothy, and Coleridge toured Scotland, De Quincey decided to
return to college, from which he had dropped out. It was
a move that Wordsworth (with whom he was already in
correspondence) thought right, but Wordsworth warned
De Quincey about the unworthy pleasures and pursuits still
to be found at the universities. He did not mean to preach,
said Wordsworth, but he warned that it was important to do
one's duty to oneself. "Love nature and books," he said, "seek
them and you will be happy."

By the end of 1807, De Quincey had met Coleridge, who
was about to lecture at the Royal Institute and, accordingly,
could not take his wife and children north on a planned visit
to the Wordsworths. There were now three Coleridge children: the remarkable Hartley, whom everyone thought a

genius; Derwent, who, his father said, had genius only in his muscles; and the fabulously beautiful little girl, Sara. Then only five years old, she was to become one of the truly intellectual women of her day.

De Quincey made a delightful escort for Mrs. Coleridge and the children, but they did not know that he was filled with panic. About to meet Wordsworth, the man who meant so much to him, he could barely contain his excitement. He felt everything, he said: agitation, restlessness, eternal self-dissatisfaction. Part of his anxiety, he realized, was just youthful exuberance, but it did not matter; it affected his body so much he trembled.

It was four o'clock when the group arrived at the Wordsworths', in time for tea. It was the most delightful meal of the day in that house, said De Quincey, because it was a time of leisure and conversation. He had never heard such speech; it gambolled and danced and played. Wordsworth spoke solemnly, majestically. Curiously enough, De Quincey's panic disappeared; the cordial welcome he had received made him feel he was in a house of superb hospitality.

And hospitable it was. At eleven, he went to bed in a pretty room measuring about fourteen feet by twelve. He realized immediately that it must be the best room in the house. In the morning he woke up to the restive sound of a child. It was John Wordsworth, Jr., then aged three, who had shared a corner of the room.

In a while there was breakfast in the little sitting room; a kettle boiled upon the fire, and the guest found the simple fare pleasing.

It was raining, but that never disturbed the Wordsworths. They took their young friend for a walk around the Lakes. The six miles they walked that day was nothing; they promised him more. They would follow Mrs. Coleridge up to her home in Keswick, where De Quincey could also meet Robert Southey. The journey would delight him.

Young Thomas knew that it was a round trip of some twenty-six miles, and he was more than a little disturbed that he would have to do it all on foot. That prospect did not bother the Coleridges or the Wordsworths, who were used to it, but De Quincey was filled with anxiety.

On the third day after his arrival in Grasmere, the whole family packed up for the expedition across the mountains. Perhaps Dorothy had sensed that the trip might be beyond the young man, because she had ordered a cart—a regular farmer's cart—and a young woman, to take them over the mountain. De Quincey, the son of a merchant, had never traveled in quite this way before, and although he had lived a bohemian life—indeed, a vagrant life—in London, he was surprised that the Wordsworths were incapable of a better carriage. What was good enough for the Wordsworths, however, was good enough for him, and so they started their trip.

De Quincey was both frightened and embarrassed; he made innumerable comments later, when he wrote down his reminiscences, that this strange party caused "no astonishments." Why should it? The Wordsworths, if they were not walking, always traveled this way, and Dorothy always hailed the stragglers on the road with warmth and affection. De Quincey was startled most of all by the young woman who was driving the cart. She would leap from the horse to the shaft of the cart like some acrobatic dancer, all the time keeping the animal well under control. And yet there were moments in which Thomas grew genuinely nervous. In the utter darkness of midnight, with lightning all about, the young woman would urge the horses to a full gallop down the narrow mountain roads, with De Quincey clutching to the sides of the cart for dear life.

They made the rest of the journey on horseback and on foot. De Quincey's arrival, just like the arrival of any stranger in the neighborhood, caused a sensation.

Southey was very hospitable. Though taller than Wordsworth, he was somewhat less commanding, but had, said Thomas, "the air of a Tyrolean mountaineer."

De Quincey could see that Wordsworth and Southey were not particularly good friends. Their actions, he felt, seemed to say, "We are too much men of sense to quarrel because we do not happen to like each other's writings. But we are neighbors, or what passes for such in the country."

Robert Southey, at that time, treated Wordsworth with a certain amount of condescension, mostly because of the latter's lack of books, and his lack of respect for those he had. The Wordsworths had only about two or three hundred books "in homely little painted bookcases on either side of the fireplace." They were ill-bound or hardly bound at all, used and re-used until they fell apart. Southey's library, on the other hand, was the most agreeable room in a house that was to become famous.

De Quincey observed that Southey had particularly elegant habits (Wordsworth called them "finical"), and some of Southey's fussiness applied to his extensive library, which he loved. Coleridge said Southey's library was his life, and Southey was known to have remarked, "To introduce Wordsworth into one's library is like letting a bear into a tulip garden."

Indeed, Wordsworth was known for taking poor care of his books. Once, when De Quincey and Wordsworth were at tea, William had picked up a volume that had just arrived from the publishers with pages still uncut, and in the excitement of seeing what the book offered, had used the butter-knife—with the butter still on the blade—to calmly cut the virgin pages. Still a creature of hero worship, Thomas was shocked.

De Quincey, who had fallen in love with the Lake District and would eventually move there, soon acquired the Words-worthian habit of walking at night. He loved to ramble end-lessly in the hazy moonlight, and even the coldness of those nocturnal walks delighted him. The valleys of Cumberland and Westmoreland were silent and solitary. He would watch the blazing fires shining through the few isolated windows. In the solitude usually reserved for owls, he would sometimes catch the sounds of household laughter. At other times, all he would hear would be the chirp of a cricket or an occasional chapel bell. Always, he liked to watch the houses dim their lights as the people inside prepared to sleep.

Southey, for his part, did less walking. He did not, said De Quincey, "have the animal spirits" that made Wordsworth such a congenial companion. William needed conversation, said De Quincey, just as Dorothy did, to throw off the state of "tumultuous excitement," to work off the excessive fervor that always seemed to be part of the poet's gift.

At that time, Greta Hall, the Southey's plain, unadorned dwelling, often held three families: Mr. Southey and his fam-ily; Mr. Coleridge and his; and the Lovell family. Mrs. Southey, Mrs. Coleridge, and Mrs. Lovell were sisters. Chil-dren abounded. But one member of the large household, the peripatetic Samuel Taylor Coleridge, was rarely present.

❧ XXI ❧

The Quarrel

All Nature seems at work. Slugs leave their lair—
The bees are stirring—birds are on the wing—
And Winter slumbering in the open air,
Wears on his smiling face a dream of Spring!
And I the while, the sole unbusy thing,
Nor honey make, nor pair, nor build, nor sing.

from: Work Without Hope
by: Samuel Taylor Coleridge

It had to come.

Now often appearing disheveled, and frequently agitated, Coleridge wrote in his journal: "Shall I ever see them again? And will it not be better that I should not? Is my body, and the habits and state of mind induced by it, such as to promise that I shall be other than a new sorrow?" Sorrow hung heavily on Coleridge, and yet he longed more than anything to see *them* again: William and Dorothy, even Mary, who now gave stability to the household, and her sister Sara Hutchinson, who drew Coleridge like a magnet.

On his return to England in August, 1806, he had not rushed to the North country, as was his custom, but had buried himself in the turmoil of London. He tried to inundate himself in work, in talk, in people. He discussed philosophy, politics, psychology, but without his former verve. His friend Charles Lamb worried about him, and asked why he did not return to Keswick to see his wife? Coleridge himself could barely understand his own reluctance. He wrote pathetic letters to his wife: "My heart aches so cruelly that I do not dare trust myself to the writing of any tenderness either to you, my dear! or to our dear children." He explained that he had just had fifty-five days of horrors. He felt he had wasted all the time he had spent in Europe and that his poetic gift was leaving him.

In utter confusion, the Wordsworths waited for him. "We have lately had much anxiety about Coleridge. What can have become of him?" they wrote. Then, later, "As the weeks went on there was still no Coleridge. Every day we may look for news of Coleridge's arrival, still Coleridge did not come."

Each week Coleridge found something new to worry about: He had to lecture; he had lost the trunk that contained gifts for Mrs. Coleridge. Every small thing took on great proportions.

The Wordsworth household had moved, for the winter, to the town of Coleorton, to Hall Farm, a house that had been lent to them by Sir George and Lady Beaumont. Coleridge must join them there; even Sara Hutchinson was waiting for him. And by all means, said the Wordsworths, he must bring his son Hartley, whom they felt was almost their own child.

Finally, after long delay, Coleridge, accompanied by Hartley, returned to the persons he needed: his dearest friends William and Dorothy; the kind Mary; and the Sara he loved so obsessively, so passionately.

Sara Hutchinson was a kind, simple person but by no means the remarkable woman Coleridge fancied her. Coleridge was excessively demanding; having lost so much, he felt he must now cling, and he clung too strongly and too bitterly to his friends. He must break with his wife, he explained to them; it was the only thing he could do. The Wordsworths looked compassionately at him, distressed by what had happened to this friend they loved. In the serenity of their household he reduced the amount of narcotics he was taking, but both he and his friends knew it was already too late. In the spring, Dorothy hoped, everything would be all right again. They would walk through the woods and the green fields, gathering primroses and honeysuckle.

But things seemed different to Coleridge. Had these people ever really understood him? Often deep friendships founder on such questions. Coleridge's own deterioration made him hypersensitive to the slightest rejection by others.

Coleridge's love for Sara "could not be hidden." He wrote disjointed, poetic love letters to her. "I must be a graceful and bold horseman, I must sing and play the harp, I must be beautiful instead of what I am, and yet she must love me for what I am, even for myself and my exceeding love." Then he added, "Oh what mad nonsense this would sound to all but myself."

Why could he not be more like Wordsworth? William, he could see, was by far the better man. He was "Greater, better, manlier, more, more dear, by nature to women than I. I, miserable I." And he brooded, too: Was not Wordsworth perhaps the greater poet? At least he was still writing productively, while Coleridge could write almost nothing.

The stability of the Wordsworth household helped him enormously, but never consistently. One day he would be in excellent spirits, writing letters to his innumerable friends all over the country, making plans for future publications. The next day he would be in bed half the day, "Often so poorly," as Dorothy said, "as to be utterly unable to do anything whatever. Today, although he came down to dinner at three perfectly well, he did not rise until near two o'clock, but however ill he may be in the mornings, he seldom fails to be cheerful and comfortable at night."

Yes, there was some comfort now for Coleridge, though he was almost beyond help. When the Wordsworths returned to Grasmere in July, 1807, to their new house, Allan Bank, William offered Coleridge a home. Knowing he should not, Coleridge nevertheless accepted—accepted not only because of his affection for William and Dorothy, but because of his

166

obsession for Sara. Just being with her meant something to him. In his room with its books, its furniture, and its shadows on the wall, slumbering with the low, quiet fire, there were within him two deeply felt feelings: love and joy. For Coleridge, merely sitting with Sara seemed to be enough. Still, his own desires, his own genius, and his insatiable need for drugs kept urging him on.

Coleridge had always enjoyed the physical production of books and magazines far more than Wordsworth. His ideas, too, were still adventuresome, and he decided that he could now pin his talents on a magazine. It would be called *The Friend,* an appropriate enough name, because Coleridge, despite his many shortcomings, still attracted friendship the way a flame attracts a moth. But Coleridge's flame fluttered; he was given now to enormous periods of procrastination. He would sputter about, pretend he was working, say that he had written page after page, though the perceptive Dorothy knew he had done nothing.

Sensing the resentment and pity of both the Wordsworths, Coleridge began to worry. How much of Sara's love was pity? Certainly she supported him spiritually. She copied his manuscripts neatly in longhand; she was actively involved in his publication schemes, and allowed the magazine to continue in a haphazard way. But eventually, even Sara grew distressed by Coleridge's demanding behavior. She knew she must leave the household.

In a way Coleridge was relieved. Dorothy, perceptive as ever, wrote "she [Sara] had, alas, no power to drive him on, and now I believe that he also is glad that she is not here." He harassed and agitated Sara's mind continually, and then, pathetically, Dorothy stated, "we have no hope for him." William was still writing industriously, but Coleridge was not

S. T. Coleridge

SAMUEL TAYLOR COLERIDGE IN OLD AGE

even interested in those parts of the poems that he himself had inspired.

The fall of 1810 started badly. Basil Montagu, Sr., an old supporter of the Wordsworths, was shocked by Coleridge's disintegration. Coleridge felt he should simply go away, to live someplace else, maybe in Edinburgh. Perhaps it would have been wise. Who knows? But the Montagus thought it still possible to reform him and asked him to live with them in London.

Meaning well, Montagu ("the most industrious creature in the world," said Dorothy, who "rises early and works late") obviously thought his influence would be helpful to the depressed Coleridge. Apparently, for a while, Coleridge was subjected even to William's moralizing, which he was ill-equipped to accept. In truth, the Wordsworths were becoming somewhat isolated, somewhat too self-absorbed, somewhat unable to look with kindness and understanding at a temperament that did not duplicate theirs.

Shortly before Coleridge was induced to leave for Montagu's house, William took Montagu aside and (so the reports that come down to us via Coleridge say) explained that Coleridge "for years past had been an *absolute* nuisance in the family." Whatever the exact words, they were harsh. Later, in his own confusion, Montagu repeated them to Coleridge.

The sensitive poet was devastated. Wordsworth's comment "had burst like a thunderstorm from a blue sky on my soul. After fifteen years of such religious, almost superstitious idolatry and self-sacrifice." For a while Coleridge's world came tumbling down. There could never be a true reconciliation. "Even if it were to be aimed for, all outward actions," wrote Coleridge, "all inward wishes, all thoughts and admirations will be the same—are the same, but—aye, there remains an unmitigable *but.*"

It was a *but* that almost affected literary history. There is no doubt that Coleridge's influence on Wordsworth during one of his most exciting periods of creativity was boundless. Some critics have even implied that Coleridge's greatest work was Wordsworth—and like all his other work, Coleridge left it unfinished. But a poet is his own creature. Wordsworth, without doubt, had flowered under the understanding and appreciative influence of Coleridge, as he had under the warm sympathy of his sister. It had been a friendship of youthful joy, and Wordsworth's poetry reflected that exhilaration in its youthful eagerness and its fresh sensations of seeing a new world. William had grown older, more serious, perhaps more priggish, but he was still a family man, still an enormously responsive and responsible human being. The Wordsworth family went on, secure with each other, no longer obsessed with the pain and anguish of one who had been "the finest friend."

❧ *XXII* ❧

A child whom every eye that looked on loved

What way does the wind come?
  What way does he go?
He rides over the water, and over the snow,
Through wood, and through vale;
  and, o'er rocky height
Which the goat cannot climb,
  takes his sounding flight;
He tosses about in every bare tree,
As, if you look up, you plainly may see;
But how he will come, and whither he goes
There's never a scholar in England knows.

from: **Address to a Child**
by: **Dorothy Wordsworth**

Dorothy, perhaps, felt the separation most. Dorothy and the children. The Wordsworth and Coleridge children had been like one family, and when Coleridge finally returned to Keswick to visit his sons, they passed the turning where Wordsworth then lived. "Poor Hartley," his mother wrote later, "sat in speechless astonishment as the chaise passed the turning to the Vicarage where W. lives, but he dared not hazard one remark, and Derwent fixed his eyes full of tears upon his father, who turned his head away to conceal his own emotions—when they had an opportunity they both eagerly asked the meaning of this paradox, and H. turned as white as lime when I told him that Mr. W. had a little vexed his father by something he had said to Montagu. . . ."

The estrangement continued, but now there was De Quincey to enjoy the children; De Quincey and Dorothy, who perhaps even more than Mary felt an extreme closeness to this household of vibrant young children. Wordsworth, of course, was fascinated by his children, who sometimes seemed to him to be words in a poem. All, that is, except for Dora, who perhaps reminded him of Dorothy when a child.

For years, Dorothy was involved in the immediate: cooking, cleaning, dressing the children, caring for them. If she wrote at all now, it was only a word or two, or maybe a little poem for their enjoyment.

De Quincey had his own ideas of enjoyment, some of them spectacular. He was now living in Dove Cottage, and on New Year's Eve, 1809, he put on a display of fireworks for all the children of the valley. Coleridge's brilliant and beautiful young daughter, Sara, was delighted. "It was like a fair," she said.

Her relationship to the Wordsworth children was, at times, difficult. Sara, who had been separated for so long from her father, could not feel instant affection toward him. For her mother, the long-suffering Mrs. Coleridge, she had a deep affection, but toward her father she felt confusion. He often reproached her, saying she was cold and did not respond affectionately, as did the Wordsworth children. In reply, she would run away and hide in the wood behind the house, where, she hoped, someone eventually would come and find her.

Young Sara was fascinated by De Quincey and sometimes, as he walked around the room talking madly with the other "room walkers" (Southey and Wordsworth), she would notice the handkerchief hanging out of De Quincey's pocket and long to clutch it. In those early years, however, nothing seemed right. Her father disliked her dresses but liked to see her wearing a cap, so the two girls, young Dora and Sara, both wore caps. The two children made a strange contrast. Dora's eyes were as wild as her aunt's; her movements were impetuous, and she had fine, long, floating yellow hair. "What am I," Sara said, "with my timid large blue eyes, muffled up in lace border and muslin?" She was bright— brighter than the rest—but lost too; and she longed for the closeness that the Wordsworths seemed to have; longed for some of the attention that De Quincey gave them.

There were now five Wordsworth children: John, the eldest, born in 1803; Dorothy, known as Dora in her father's poems, born in 1804; Thomas, born in 1806; Catherine, born in 1808, and the baby, William, born in 1810. Each child had his own individuality. Johnny, to whom De Quincey sent presents from London, could be taught to swim, fly a kite, sail a boat. Little Catherine, to De Quincey, seemed the gayest of all; even physically, she appeared different from the other children. Wordsworth called her a Chinese maiden; De Quincey simply called her "Kate Beautiful." Kate and young Thomas suffered from poor health. In the years when it was difficult to raise an entire family to adulthood, there was always anxiety about the simplest childhood diseases; indeed, the entire Wordsworth household at that time had health problems. William's eyes seemed to be constantly failing him; he developed boils on his body; and his writing, possibly because of Coleridge's lack of support, seemed to go slower and slower. Dorothy and Mary were prey to colds: the damp walks they enjoyed so often left them with unidentified aches and pains—but never would they hear a word against the erratic weather of their Lake Country.

The Wordsworth family had settled down to a kind of routine, the routine of living in the vales. Clannish, dependent upon one another, London and the Continent seemed far away. Although Napoleon and the war were topics of conversation, and although Wordsworth worked on a political pamphlet that De Quincey helped him publish, the center of Wordsworth's life, its heart, was in the Lake District.

Throughout the area there were remote dales having little communication with the outside world. There were high hills with not even a sheep track or a shepherd's house on them. "Nothing but rock and heath, rock and heath," as De Quincey said, "in monotonous confusion." One such dale was called Far Easedale, a chain of everlasting hills where the climb across the mountain was perhaps some twenty miles. Even in midday it appeared a long valley of utter desolation. Here, in one of these bleak spots, lived George and Sara Greene with their small children.

The Greenes were well known to the Wordsworths; they were a respectable family, and the children went to the Grasmere school. There was little entertainment for the parents in the valley, except for frequent sales or auctions. Thus, on a very cold, snowy day, Mrs. Greene, loathe to miss one, went with her husband to such an auction. They had left their six children at home, one an infant at the breast, all of them under twelve years old.

That evening, the children waited patiently for their parents' return. Tired and hungry, but familiar as they were with the bad weather of the Lake District, they felt at the beginning no real fright. The oldest of the girls, Sally, was working at the moment for the Wordsworths, so it was up to Agnes, just nine years old, to comfort the younger ones as well as she could. She was able to keep the peat fire going, and she kept herself awake as the moon rose over the fells.

The following morning she was deeply worried; there had been a heavy snowfall, and the children were literally imprisoned. There was no one with whom they could communicate, as neighbors were few and far between. By evening, the children were huddled around the hearth, thinking that perhaps their parents were in real danger—or even dead. Death came easily to people in the fells, and only recently an old man had fallen and died of exposure. Months later searchers found him and his dog, for the dog never left his master's side in winter.

Children grew up with these terrors and the knowledge that the mountains were dangerous. Prayer might help, and little Agnes prayed. At the same time, she tried to be as practical as possible. She carefully wound the clock so she would know what time it was. She took the little milk that was left —it was the cheapest, called "blue milk," a kind of skim milk—and scalded it so it would not turn sour. Like a good administrator, she started to ration the food and cooked only small portions of porridge. She searched to find a few potatoes, and stacked the little peat that was left so the fire could be kept burning. Then she tried to milk a cow, but it gave little milk. Agnes, herself such a young child, grew more and more frightened. Sometimes she thought she heard the sound of voices, sometimes cries; she could not tell.

The children looked out and saw that the snow was drifting heavily. Their parents had been gone more than three days. In spite of the drifts, there seemed to be a slight path; perhaps Agnes could walk to Grasmere. Eventually she made the attempt, making her way to the nearest house, the Wordsworths'. When she arrived, she was in tears.

The news sped through the valley, De Quincey said, "like fire in an American forest." Search parties went out, but after five days Mr. and Mrs. Greene had still not been found. However, the dalesmen never gave up. When one of the men came in, Dorothy Wordsworth would give him coffee and ask, "What will you do now?" "Go up again, of course," would be the reply.

Men and dogs kept climbing through the thick vapor until the bodies were found. Misled by blinding snow, threatened by the precipices, husband and wife had apparently died on that first cold night.

Dorothy and William did everything they could to find new homes for the children. They themselves kept Sally, the oldest. De Quincey had never liked her and later blamed her

GRASMERE CHURCH

Illustration by Joseph Pennell

bitterly for another tragedy. Although young and ignorant,
she nonetheless made a nursemaid of sorts for the youngest of
the Wordsworth children, whose demands were ever increas-
ing.

The family moved into the Allan Bank rectory, and life
was very busy. The hay had to be taken in and men were
needed to work in the fields. For Dorothy, life seemed to be
a constant round of making beds, cooking, paying attention
to the children. Dora would be going to boarding school
soon. Her manners were not what they should be, but she
was a lovely girl. It was the baby, Kate Beautiful, they worried
about.

It was Sally's fault, De Quincey wrote later, that Kate
Beautiful became ill. Supposedly, Sally had allowed young
Catherine to eat her fill of raw carrots; in any case the child
"did indulge in them and rapidly came down with convulsions." We surmise now that there was probably some physi-

cal birth defect in Catherine that caused her attack, leaving her left side, her left arm, and her left leg paralyzed, so that she walked in a crawling fashion. The child loved De Quincey deeply, and he loved her. She was, he said, "at my solitary cottage often my sole companion." At that time Catherine was barely three years old, but she was "a blithe society," who evoked "gladness and involuntary songs," her father said.

Worried about Catherine, they worried, too, about young Thomas. Trips to the seashore did not help the invalids. On December 2, 1812, Thomas died of measles. The household was once again consumed with grief. Dorothy had been away for a short visit. When she returned, she found Mary exhausted but still the strength of the family, coping with her own grief as well as comforting all the others.

The adults often longed to get away from the isolation of the vale. Mary's health had been impaired again, and she went off to visit her brother in the early summer. In the meantime, William went to London, eager to do whatever he could to heal the rift with Coleridge.

The weather was beautiful; Catherine seemed to be healthy and in joyous spirits. In the middle of the night young John went to get his aunt Dorothy. Catherine had a strange look in her eyes, he said. By morning she was dead. Dorothy was disconsolate.

The family had to move; everything now held some remembrance of the children who had died. They would go to a house called Rydal Mount. From there they could see the Grasmere hills they always loved. There, Mary's good spirits would return. The only bright spot now was a letter from Coleridge, who wrote them in consolation. "Our sorrow," said Dorothy, "has sunk into him and he loved the darling the best of all our little ones." Still, Coleridge did not visit.

A child whom every eye that looked on loved

In the graveyard at Grasmere, the tombstones bear the lines Wordsworth wrote for his children, children whom "every eye that looked on loved."

The family, jaded with fatigue and grief, prepared to move into Rydal Mount. Perhaps the bustle of getting settled would help them.

❧ *XXIII* ❧

This will never do

Farewell, thou little Nook of mountain-ground,
Thou rocky corner in the lowest stair
Of that magnificent temple which doth bound
One side of our whole vale with grandeur rare;
Sweet garden-orchard, eminently fair,
The loveliest spot that man hath ever found,
Farewell!—we leave thee to Heaven's peaceful care,
Thee, and the Cottage which thou dost surround.

from: A Farewell
by: William Wordsworth

"We are going to have a *Turkey!!!* carpet—in the dining-room," Dorothy wrote to her friend Catherine Clarkson, "and a Brussels in William's study. You stare, and the simplicity of the dear Town End Cottage comes before your eyes, and you are tempted to say, 'are they changed, are they setting up for fine Folks? for making parties—giving Dinners, etc. etc.?' "

It did not appear to Dorothy, William, and Mary that they had changed very much, but of course they had. They were all getting older. They could not live forever in a cottage, nor could they live forever with little money. It was becoming obvious to William that he must have some other employment than that of a poet, and, accordingly, he used what influence he had to become a civil servant, a Distributor of Stamps. This was a wide-ranging post that brought monies from such diverse activities as the granting of licenses for the selling of medicines to the imposing of taxes on "persons letting to hire Stage Coaches." The position brought him a small income of roughly two hundred pounds a year that helped sustain him throughout the rest of his life.

William's moods changed, depending upon his work: politics disturbed him, any threat to his children's health made him frantic. But he loved to joke, and it was said that he was "always the soul of the parties abroad." Still, there were times when only poetry could interest him. "William, in the midst of all this bustle is busy among his verses—and only agreeable by fits," Sara Hutchinson said. At other times, she complained, "He lives only for himself and his books."

All poets, indeed all writers, lead a kind of split life: one within their home and with their friends; the other the private life of the writer, the poet. The solitary individual, the spectator, the person apart, always inspired Wordsworth. All his "solitaries," as he called them, were strange, unusual persons whom he had seen in his walks and rambles around the country.

The long poem Wordsworth wanted to write, "a narrative poem of the epic kind," was to be called *The Recluse*. It was never completed; but *The Prelude,* finally published after his death, was the introduction to that great work. *The Prelude,* however, stands as an epic itself. It was not only an introduction to the unfinished poem, but an introduction to a new kind of writing. It is also one of the great autobiographies of literature "for," said Wordsworth, "a poet's writing was his biography." In *The Prelude* he looks back through older eyes at his own childhood, a period of unbelievable richness.

"Only through time, time is conquered," he once wrote. His thoughts and discussions of time, his time-consciousness were one of the revolutionary aspects of his work. It was not really until the twentieth century that *The Prelude* was understood to be the great poem it is, for it was in this century that such great writers as James Joyce and Marcel Proust let their minds roam back and forth with a new understanding of time. The action of a novel, Joyce explained, could take place in a single day. A man like Proust could spend a lifetime recreating remembrances of time past. So, as the world moved into the twentieth century, *The Prelude* came into its own; and as the world moves once again toward a new century, with young persons demanding a new individuality, a better, more natural world, Wordsworth speaks afresh.

In his own day, from the publication of *The Lyrical Ballads* with Coleridge, through his middle years, Wordsworth always had a limited audience. Perhaps one could say that he wanted no other audience than the one he needed: Dorothy and Coleridge. But good poets do strive for some audience, and William, of course, always tried for publication. *The Lyrical Ballads* had made little money and his other volumes, as they were published, made less. Indeed, they appeared to make enemies because Wordsworth's voice was too new, too solitary, too different. He was in the *avant-garde* of the poetry of his day.

"This will never do." That was the beginning of a review of one of Wordsworth's poems in the influential *Edinburgh Review*. It has gone down in literary history as one of the more ridiculous clichés of reviewing. Arrogant and stupid, it was a phrase written by a man in his own private rage about a poet he did not choose to understand. Wordsworth accepted such attacks with reasonably good grace. If a friend suggested a change William might sometimes consider it but, as a whole, he admired his own poetry, sometimes to a degree that irritated his London friends, whom he now saw more frequently.

But as he endlessly corrected and changed *The Prelude*, there were fewer new poems. It was a time for settling in, and in some ways Wordsworth settled in too strongly. He, who had been almost a radical in his youth, became extremely conservative politically.

Other things were changing, too: his reputation, for instance. He was, at last, beginning to be genuinely well known. Many of the young looked upon him as the great voice of the Romantic Movement. It was he who had first extolled the pleasure of the senses, the delight in the vision of the natural world—its sounds, its comforts, its vicissitudes. To enjoy nature, to respond to it—indeed, just to be able to respond to it —showed, thought Wordsworth, the "rightness" of life. And Dorothy and Coleridge agreed.

The younger John Keats admired Wordsworth and was even influenced by him. Keats would go on to extol the senses with a greater depth, an even richer immediacy than Wordsworth. By the time they met there was the gap that always exists between literary generations, though Keats, as a boy, had been greatly excited when Benjamin Robert Haydon, a painter and friend of Keats's, suggested sending one of Keats's poems to Wordsworth: "The idea of your sending it to Wordsworth puts me out of breath—you know with what reverence I would send my well wishes to him."

But the gap was there. When Keats recited his poem "Hymn to Pan," Wordsworth had difficulty in recognizing a new voice: "a pretty piece of paganism," he called it. Yes, Wordsworth had changed. Even his clothes were different. A contemporary account tells us: "When Keats first called on Wordsworth he was kept waiting for a long time, and when Wordsworth entered, he was in full flower, knee breeches, silk stockings, etc., and in a great hurry as he was going to dine with one of the Commissioners of Stamps."

The private poet had turned into the public man.

❧ *XXIV* ❧

From sunshine to the sunless land

There was a time when meadow, grove, and stream,
The earth, and every common sight,
   To me did seem
   Apparelled in celestial light,
The glory and the freshness of a dream.
It is not now as it hath been of yore;—
   Turn wheresoe'er I may,
   By night or day,
The things which I have seen I now can see no more.

from: **Ode: Intimations of Immortality**
from Recollections of Early Childhood
by: **William Wordsworth**

"Rydal Mount," wrote Dorothy, "is the nicest place in the world for children. You would almost long to be young again, as I do, when you see it; for the sake of trotting down the green banks, running and dancing on the mount, etc. You must come and see us, indeed you must before it is too late for you and all of us."

Dorothy, as she watched the children grow up, felt the world closing in upon her. There were so many personal things to worry about: her teeth, for example, which, with the exception of three above and three below, were all gone now.

The appearances of her friends had also changed. Mary Lamb had lost only one tooth, but she had become "sadly fat and dresses so loose that she looks the worst for it, yet she is still a good walker." No matter how the years had changed Dorothy, they did not change her ability to walk or her inclination to wander. She traveled farther afield now, not only visiting throughout England, but even making one trip to France after the marriage of Caroline, Annette and William's daughter, to a young French civil servant named Jean-Baptiste Baudoin.

In London, where Dorothy went whenever she could, she liked the solitary walks and the occasional garden with one lone, rustic cow grazing. She loved the Thames, with its water at that time still as clear and as bright as the water of the lakes. She delighted in boating trips on the river, "a shilling's worth on the water," she said.

When William or Mary took off for brief visits, Dorothy frequently stayed at Rydal, watching whatever young person was home or on vacation from school. John had already taken his degree at Oxford. Willy, who was not drawn to the academic life, planned to enter the army. Dorothy, as usual, recorded the family reaction: "I am sure that there will be no turning him from it, and his poor mother will be wretched when she finds this out to be the case, because neither Mary nor William like Willy's army fever."

By the summer of 1828, the sounds of children's voices had vanished from Rydal Mount. The young people had all disappeared. Dora, William's favorite, was in Germany with him and Coleridge, a glorious trip for all because finally Wordsworth and Coleridge had become reconciled (at least partially —there was still some irritation).

Dora, in a letter to her mother, wrote: "They get on famously, but Mr. C. sometimes detains us with his fiddle-faddling, and he likes prosing to the folks better than exerting himself to see the face of the country and Father with his few half-dozen words of German makes himself much better understood than Mr. C. with all his weight of German literature."

A traveler, Thomas Gratton, left a penned portrait of both Coleridge and Wordsworth as they journeyed through the Rhine Valley. Coleridge was "about five feet five inches in height, of a full and lazy appearance, but not actually stout. He was dressed in black and wore short breeches, buttoned and tied at the knees and black silk stockings. . . . His face was extremely handsome, its expression placid and benevolent, his mouth was particularly pleasing and his soft gray eyes, neither large nor prominent were full of intelligent softness. His hair of which he had plenty was entirely white, his forehead and cheeks were unfurrowed and the latter showed a healthy bloom. Wordsworth was a complete antithesis to Coleridge, tall, wiry, harsh in features, coarse in figure, inelegant in looks. He was roughly dressed in long brown surtout, striped duck trousers, fustian gaiters and thick shoes. He more resembled a mountain farmer than a lake poet. His whole air was unrefined and unprepossessing. He seemed satisfied to let his friend and fellow take the lead with a want of pretension rarely found in men of literary reputation, far inferior to his, while there was something unobtrusively amiable in his bearing toward his daughter."

As Coleridge wandered around on his visit to the Continent he used to say that the aphorism "the more we have seen, the less we have to say" is only too true. In youth, the mind and the nature are two different things, rival artists, semi-potent magicians. Youth makes it easier to paint the canvas, to put the pen to paper. But even writers get older. Nature itself, said Coleridge, is a "warily, wily, long-breathed old witch, tough-lived as a turtle. She transforms the canvas into a color of dullness, all life itself gets a little less exciting."

Now Coleridge and Wordsworth were both famous. Coleridge remained the indefatigable talker. After returning from their trip to the Continent, he and Wordsworth were not to see each other except upon rare occasions. Sometimes there would be talks between them about Coleridge's son Hartley, who seemed to have the same self-destructive tendencies as his father.

"Can anything be more dreadful than the thought that an innocent child has inherited from you a disease or a weakness, the penalty in yourself of sin or want of caution?" Coleridge asked.

It was true that young Hartley was very much a bohemian,

Wm Wordsworth

disappearing on and off over the years, while Derwent, the other son, was often criticized by Coleridge for his social activities.

As the years moved on, Coleridge talked more and more. Wordsworth once visited him, or so the story goes, and nodded his head for two hours at the continuous chain of conversation.

"Could you understand what Coleridge was saying?" he was asked later.

"Not a word," replied Wordsworth.

The children on Coleridge's street began to think him a little curious. He used such long words that the young people were puzzled and hid behind trees, peering out at him, occasionally giving a wild hoot. He talked of everything: of chemistry, of colors, of Newton, of grammar, of the new poetry, of Schlegel and Goethe. He was still subject to great physical discomfort and had to walk up and down in the Highgate home of the Gilman's, where he now lived, to ease his pain. He thought more and more of those happy days with the Wordsworths and with Charles and Mary Lamb.

Dr. James Gilman and his wife Anne, who had given Coleridge a home, continued to enjoy his company. He was kind to the household help, was "a most engaging home companion," and "the gentlest and kindest teacher."

Coleridge himself knew time was moving on; he was writing his own epitaph now. Nevertheless, his death on July 25, 1834, came as an enormous shock to Wordsworth, who said: "It is nearly forty years since I first became acquainted with him whom we have just lost; and though with the exception of six weeks when we were on the Continent together, along with my daughter, I have seen little of him for the last twenty years, his mind has been habitually present with me, with an accompanying feeling that he was still in the flesh.

That frail tie is broken, and I and most of those who are nearest and dearest to me must prepare and endeavor to follow him."

His words were almost too true. The following December came the word of the death of Charles Lamb, and Mary Lamb was institutionalized again.

Dorothy became increasingly ill. "Her loving kindness has no bounds," wrote her brother. "God bless her for ever and ever." She recovered, only to grow ill once more. Her perception about the world was to sharpen again, however, and she turned to her Journal in the new year of 1835 and wrote: "Never surely in the 63 years that I have lived can there have been two such brilliant New Years and Christmas days. . . . Another year begun! and what a brilliant sunrise—oh! That men's hearts could be *softened!* and elevated by the goodness and beauty of all that is done for and spread around us!"

She also wrote a poem:

> *Joy is brought to my* hidden *life,*
> *To consciousness no longer hidden.* . . .

By the spring of that year, Dora, Dorothy, and Sara Hutchinson were attacked by influenza. Dora recovered; gentle Sara died; Dorothy appeared to rally. Although Dorothy lived, she was never again the same, her mind was never again lucid.

William felt they were all going—his supporters and his friends. He wrote a dirge for Coleridge, for Scott, now dead, and for Lamb:

> *The mighty Minstrel breathes no longer,*
> *'Mid mouldering ruins low he lies;*
> *And death upon the braes of Yarrow*
> *Has closed the Shepherd-poet's eyes:*
>
> *Nor has the rolling year twice measured,*
> *From sign to sign, its steadfast course,*

Dorothy and William Wordsworth

Since every mortal power of Coleridge
Was frozen at its marvelous source;

The rapt One, of the godlike forehead,
The heaven-eyed creature sleeps in earth:
And Lamb, the frolic and the gentle,
Has vanished from his lonely hearth.

Like clouds that rake the mountain-summits,
Or waves that own no curbing hand,

From sunshine to the sunless land

How fast has brother followed brother,
From sunshine to the sunless land.

His daughter, dear Dora, left him to marry Edward Quil-linan—a marriage Wordsworth felt was beneath her. She and her husband traveled constantly in an effort to improve her health, but the trips were to no avail. They returned to Rydal Mount in 1847. It was here that Dora died on July 9.

For William, the only sunshine remaining in a sunless land was Mary's warmth, the satisfaction of waiting upon Dorothy, and sitting with her in front of a great fire. The world outside knew him for a great man—a great poet—but inside this house he was Dorothy's brother. Her mind, which had once been for him a "mansion," was now only a deserted hut. Yet she would outlive him. Once, in a rational moment, she said to a visitor: "My brothers were all good men, good, good! The boys in our family were all good, *I* was always the terma-gant. . . ."

The wild one—and the muse.

❧ XXV ❧

The Poetry of Earth

Then sing, ye Birds, sing, sing, a joyous song!
  And let the young Lambs bound
  As to the tabor's sound!
We in thought will join your throng,
  Ye that pipe and ye that play,
  Ye that through your hearts today
  Feel the gladness of the May!

from: Ode: Intimations of Immortality
from Recollections of Early Childhood
by: William Wordsworth

The villagers stood around the house and watched the shadows move within the room; then, finally, the curtains were drawn. Wordsworth was dead. The group dispersed, knowing they had lost a good neighbor, a good friend, and, perhaps, even a man of genius. But it was not his genius that concerned them; it was that he always had had a kind word for those around him, and that he had immortalized their own countryside. He was, at heart, a local boy.

His very era was to be called the "Age of Wordsworth," and it was one of the greatest ages of poetry. William had become the Poet Laureate of England after the death of Robert Southey, in 1843. He had become a famous man to whom persons from all over the world made a pilgrimage. But always he had been a man who had loved his land, who had time to plant trees and notice the wildflowers, who was concerned with the green beauty of the countryside.

For the world at large he would always be linked with two other figures: his sister Dorothy and Samuel Taylor Coleridge. The "Age of Wordsworth" actually belonged to all three. William Wordsworth died on April 23—Shakespeare's birthday—and on that day, in 1850, the land was covered with foliage.

Keats was to write: "The poetry of earth is never dead," and certainly this is true, too, of the poets of our earth, particularly those who give us a new way of looking at the ever-changing seasons and our ever-changing land. Today Wordsworth is considered one of the greatest of all poets—and one of the most modern. His concern, and Dorothy's, and Samuel's, for the land gives them a new voice.

The Lake District of England has now been preserved as a National Park. In any springtime, on those April days they extolled so well, one can walk with these three friends. One can follow them: Coleridge, always talking not only of poetry and the spirit, but of the land itself; Dorothy sitting under the holly tree that grew upon the rock, watching joyfully as William, a little apart, flings stones into the river, which roars with an immortality all its own.

Yes, one can walk with them, sharing what Dorothy used to call "a feast of silence." One can sit and listen to what they called "the voice of the air," and see them relaxing on the grass, listening to the peaceful sounds of the earth.

They understood the earth in the way that we are just now beginning to understand it—with a desire to stop the reckless destruction of the land. Coleridge and William and Dorothy Wordsworth felt that the study of nature not only fed the mind, but also nourished the spirit and the senses.

They conversed with nature, as well as with books and with one another. And nature, too, taught them their art, for there was design in it and there had to be design in art—design and hard work. Yes, there was spontaneity, but there was something more, something that Wordsworth called "love for my art. I therefore labor at it with reverence, affection, and industry."

They allowed their minds to roam freely and gently among all the flowering plants of life and the imagination. The way they looked upon even their changing world—they had the same threats of an encroaching technology as we do now—

had a freshness to it. Once, for example, when Wordsworth. Coleridge, and Dorothy were walking together in Scotland, they saw a steam engine—still something new to the countryside—and Wordsworth said that one immediately got the impression it had a life and volition of its own. "Yes," replied Coleridge, "it is a giant with but one idea."

These three friends were not persons of one idea but of many. Nature has a freedom about it, an ever-changing pattern. Even for today's artist, hemmed in by a world of technology, nature still provides a sense of new-found freedom.

It was the land that taught the Wordsworths and Coleridge, and indeed that teaches most poets, that there is always another tomorrow, always a new season, when daffodils will grow again, a tomorrow to which each of us can make a contribution. Once, when William climbed to the highest rock on one of his favorite crags, he pulled some berries from a holly tree and carried them up to a naked spot of soil to plant them there. "I like to do this for posterity," he said. "Some people are selfish enough to say, 'what has posterity done for me?' But the past does much for us."

The past has given us poets we can enjoy forever, a way of looking at the world that often neatly dovetails with some of the changing patterns of our own time. The past sometimes appears simple, but "the Age of Wordsworth" was really no simpler than our present age; the threats were there, the wars were there, the same human conflicts were there. Today, nature is as alien to some people as books are to others, but Wordsworth said, "love nature and books." It is a happy combination.

A Wordsworth
❧ Sampler ❦

GRASMERE LOOKING TOWARDS DUNMAIL RAISE

"When I first came with William, six and a half years ago, it was just at sunset, there was a rich yellow light on the waters, and the islands were reflected there; today it was grave and soft."

—Dorothy Wordsworth

Dorothy Wordsworth's Journal, written at Alfoxden in 1798

ALFOXDEN, *January 20th, 1798.* The green paths down the hill-sides are channels for streams. The young wheat is streaked by silver lines of water running between the ridges, the sheep are gathered together on the slopes. After the wet dark days, the country seems more populous. It peoples itself in the sunbeams. The garden, mimic of spring, is gay with flowers. The purple-starred hepatica spreads itself in the sun, and the clustering snow-drops put forth their white heads, at first upright, ribbed with green, and like a rosebud when completely opened, hanging their heads downward, but slowly lengthening their slender stems. The slanting woods of an unvarying brown, showing the light through the thin network of their upper boughs. Upon the highest ridge of that round hill covered with planted oaks, the shafts of the trees show in the light like the columns of a ruin.

January 21st. Walked on the hill-tops—a warm day. Sate under the firs in the park. The tops of the beeches of a brown-red, or crimson. Those oaks, fanned by the sea breeze, thick with feathery sea-green moss, as a grove not stripped of its leaves. Moss cups more proper than acorns for fairy goblets.

January 22nd. Walked through the wood to Holford. The ivy twisting round the oaks like bristled serpents. The day cold—a warm shelter in the hollies, capriciously bearing berries. Query: Are the male and female flowers on separate trees?

January 23rd. Bright sunshine, went out at 3 o'clock. The sea perfectly calm blue, streaked with deeper colour by the clouds, and tongues or points of sand; on our return of a gloomy red. The sun gone down. The crescent moon, Jupiter, and Venus. The sound of the sea distinctly heard on the tops of the hills, which we could never hear in summer. We attribute this partly to the bareness of the trees, but chiefly to the absence of the singing of birds, the hum of insects, that noiseless noise which lives in the summer air. The villages marked out by beautiful beds of smoke. The turf fading into the mountain road. The scarlet flowers of the moss.

January 24th. Walked between half-past three and half-past five. The evening cold and clear. The sea of a sober grey, streaked by the deeper grey clouds. The half dead sound of the near sheep-bell, in the hollow of the sloping coombe, exquisitely soothing.

January 25th. Went to Poole's after tea. The sky spread over with one continuous cloud, whitened by the light of the moon, which, though her dim shape was seen, did not throw forth so strong a light as to chequer the earth with shadows. At once the clouds seemed to cleave asunder, and left her in the centre of a black-blue vault. She sailed along, followed by multitudes of stars, small, and bright, and sharp. Their brightness seemed concentrated (half-moon).

January 26th. Walked upon the hill-tops; followed the

sheep tracks till we overlooked the larger coombe. Sat in the sunshine. The distant sheep-bells, the sound of the stream; the woodman winding along the half-marked road with his laden pony; locks of wool still spangled with the dewdrops; the blue-grey sea, shaded with immense masses of cloud, not streaked; the sheep glittering in the sunshine. Returned through the wood. The trees skirting the wood, being exposed more directly to the action of the sea breeze, stripped of the net-work of their upper boughs, which are stiff and erect, like black skeletons; the ground strewed with the red berries of the holly. Set forward before two o'clock. Returned a little after four.

January 27th. Walked from seven o'clock till half-past eight. Upon the whole an uninteresting evening. Only once while we were in the wood the moon burst through the invisible veil which enveloped her, the shadows of the oaks blackened, and their lines became more strongly marked. The withered leaves were coloured with a deeper yellow, a brighter gloss spotted the hollies; again her form became dimmer; the sky flat, unmarked by distances, a white thin cloud. The manufacturer's dog makes a strange, uncouth howl, which it continues many minutes after there is no noise near it but that of the brook. It howls at the murmur of the village stream.

January 28th. Walked only to the mill.

January 29th. A very stormy day. William walked to the top of the hill to see the sea. Nothing distinguishable but a heavy blackness. An immense bough riven from one of the fir trees.

January 30th. William called me into the garden to observe a singular appearance about the moon. A perfect rainbow, within the bow one star, only of colours more vivid. The semi-circle soon became a complete circle, and in the course of three or four minutes the whole faded away. Walked to the blacksmith's and the baker's; an uninteresting evening.

January 31st. Set forward to Stowey at half-past five. A violent storm in the wood; sheltered under the hollies. When we left home the moon immensely large, the sky scattered over with clouds. These soon closed in, contracting the dimensions of the moon without concealing her. The sound of the pattering shower, and the gusts of wind, very grand. Left the wood when nothing remained of the storm but the driving wind, and a few scattering drops of rain. Presently all clear, Venus first showing herself between the struggling clouds; afterwards Jupiter appeared. The hawthorn hedges, black and pointed, glittering with millions of diamond drops; the hollies shining with broader patches of light. The road to the village of Holford glittered like another stream. On our return, the wind high—a violent storm of hail and rain at the Castle of Comfort. All the Heavens seemed in one perpetual motion when the rain ceased; the moon appearing, now half veiled, and now retired behind heavy clouds, the stars still moving, the roads very dirty.

February 1st. About two hours before dinner, set forward towards Mr. Bartholemew's.[1] The wind blew so keen in our faces that we felt ourselves inclined to seek the covert of the wood. There we had a warm shelter, gathered a burthen of large rotten boughs blown down by the wind of the preceding night. The sun shone clear, but all at once a heavy blackness hung over the sea. The trees almost *roared,* and the ground seemed in motion with the multitudes of dancing leaves, which made a rustling sound, distinct from that of the trees. Still the asses pastured in quietness under the hollies, undisturbed by these forerunners of the storm. The wind beat furiously against us as we returned. Full moon. She rose in uncommon majesty over the sea, slowly ascending through the clouds. Sat with the window open an hour in the moonlight.

[1] Mr. Bartholemew rented Alfoxden, and sublet the house to Wordsworth.

February 2nd. Walked through the wood, and on to the Downs before dinner; a warm pleasant air. The sun shone, but was often obscured by straggling clouds. The redbreasts made a ceaseless song in the woods. The wind rose very high in the evening. The room smoked so that we were obliged to quit it. Young lambs in a green pasture in the Coombe, thick legs, large heads, black staring eyes.

February 3rd. A mild morning, the windows open at breakfast, the redbreasts singing in the garden. Walked with Coleridge over the hills. The sea at first obscured by vapour; that vapour afterwards slid in one mighty mass along the sea-shore; the islands and one point of land clear beyond it. The distant country (which was purple in the clear dull air), overhung by straggling clouds that sailed over it, appeared like the darker clouds, which are often seen at a great distance apparently motionless, while the nearer ones pass quickly over them, driven by the lower winds. I never saw such a union of earth, sky, and sea. The clouds beneath our feet spread themselves to the water, and the clouds of the sky almost joined them. Gathered sticks in the wood; a perfect stillness. The redbreasts sang upon the leafless boughs. Of a great number of sheep in the field, only one standing. Returned to dinner at five o'clock. The moonlight still and warm as a summer's night at nine o'clock.

February 4th. Walked a great part of the way to Stowey with Coleridge. The morning warm and sunny. The young lasses seen on the hill-tops, in the villages and roads, in their summer holiday clothes—pink petticoats and blue. Mothers with their children in arms, and the little ones that could just walk, tottering by their side. Midges or small flies spinning in the sunshine; the songs of the lark and redbreast; daisies upon the turf; the hazels in blossom; honeysuckles budding. I saw one solitary strawberry flower under a hedge. The furze gay with blossom. The moss rubbed from the pailings by the sheep, that leave locks of wool, and the red marks with which they are spotted, upon the wood.

February 5th. Walked to Stowey with Coleridge, returned by Woodlands; a very warm day. In the continued singing of birds distinguished the notes of a blackbird or thrush. The sea overshadowed by a thick dark mist, the land in sunshine. The sheltered oaks and beeches still retaining their brown leaves. Observed some trees putting out red shoots. Query: What trees are they?

February 6th. Walked to Stowey over the hills, returned to tea, a cold and clear evening, the roads in some parts frozen hard. The sea hid by mist all the day.

February 7th. Turned towards Potsham, but finding the way dirty, changed our course. Cottage gardens the object of our walk. Went up the smaller Coombe to Woodlands, to the blacksmith's, the baker's, and through the village of Holford. Still misty over the sea. The air very delightful. We saw nothing very new, or interesting.

February 8th. Went up the Park, and over the tops of the hills, till we came to a new and very delicious pathway, which conducted us to the Coombe. Sat a considerable time upon the heath. Its surface restless and glittering with the motion of the scattered piles of withered grass, and the waving of the spiders' threads. On our return the mist still hanging over the sea, but the opposite coast clear, and the rocky cliffs distinguishable. In the deep Coombe, as we stood upon the sunless hill, we saw miles of grass, light and glittering, and the insects passing.

February 9th. William gathered sticks. . . .

February 10th. Walked to Woodlands, and to the waterfall. The adder's-tongue and the ferns green in the low damp dell. These plants now in perpetual motion from the current of the air; in summer only moved by the drippings of the rocks. A cloudy day.

February 11th. Walked with Coleridge near to Stowey. The day pleasant, but cloudy.

February 12th. Walked alone to Stowey. Returned in the evening with Coleridge. A mild, pleasant, cloudy day.

February 13th. Walked with Coleridge through the wood. A mild and pleasant morning, the near prospect clear. The ridges of the hills fringed with wood, showing the sea through them like the white sky, and still beyond the dim horizon of the distant hills, hanging as it were in one undetermined line between sea and sky.

February 14th. Gathered sticks with William in the wood, he being unwell and not able to go further. The young birch trees of a bright red, through which gleams a shade of purple. Sat down in a thick part of the wood. The near trees still, even to their topmost boughs, but a perpetual motion in those that skirt the wood. The breeze rose gently; its path distinctly marked, till it came to the very spot where we were.

February 15th. Gathered sticks in the further wood. The dell green with moss and brambles, and the tall and slender pillars of the unbranching oaks. I crossed the water with letters; returned to Wm. and Basil.[1] A shower met us in the wood, and a ruffling breeze.

February 16th. Went for eggs into the Coombe, and to the baker's; a hail shower; brought home large burthens of sticks, a starlight evening, the sky closed in, and the ground white with snow before we went to bed.

February 17th. A deep snow upon the ground. Wm. and Coleridge walked to Mr. Bartholemew's, and to Stowey. Wm. returned, and we walked through the wood into the Coombe to fetch some eggs. The sun shone bright and clear. A deep stillness in the thickest part of the wood, undisturbed except by the occasional dropping of the snow from the holly boughs; no other sound but that of the water, and the slender notes

[1] The little son of W.'s friend Montagu.

of a redbreast, which sang at intervals on the outskirts of the southern side of the wood. There the bright green moss was bare at the roots of the trees, and the little birds were upon it. The whole appearance of the wood was enchanting; and each tree, taken singly, was beautiful. The branches of the hollies pendent with their white burden, but still showing their bright red berries, and their glossy green leaves. The bare branches of the oaks thickened by the snow.

February 18th. Walked after dinner beyond Woodlands.[2] A sharp and very cold evening; first observed the crescent moon, a silvery line, a thready bow, attended by Jupiter and Venus in their palest hues.

February 19th. I walked to Stowey before dinner; Wm. unable to go all the way. Returned alone; a fine sunny, clear, frosty day. The sea still, and blue, and broad, and smooth.

February 20th. Walked after dinner towards Woodlands.

February 21st. Coleridge came in the morning, which prevented our walking. Wm. went through the wood with him towards Stowey; a very stormy night.

February 22nd. Coleridge came in the morning to dinner. Wm. and I walked after dinner to Woodlands; the moon and two planets; sharp and frosty. Met a razor-grinder with a soldier's jacket on, a knapsack upon his back, and a boy to drag his wheel. The sea very black, and making a loud noise as we came through the wood, loud as if disturbed, and the wind was silent.

February 23rd. William walked with Coleridge in the morning. I did not go out.

February 24th. Went to the hill-top. Sat a considerable time overlooking the country towards the sea. The air blew pleasantly round us. The landscape mildly interesting. The Welsh

2 This house was afterwards John Kenyon's—to whom *Aurora Leigh* is dedicated—and was subsequently the residence of the Rev. William Nichols, author of *The Quantocks and Their Associations*.

hills capped by a huge range of tumultuous white clouds. The sea, spotted with white, of a bluish grey in general, and streaked with darker lines. The near shores clear; scattered farm houses, half-concealed by green mossy orchards, fresh straw lying at the doors; hay-stacks in the fields. Brown fallows, the springing wheat, like a shade of green over the brown earth, and the choice meadow plots, full of sheep and lambs, of a soft and vivid green; a few wreaths of blue smoke, spreading along the ground; the oaks and beeches in the hedges retaining their yellow leaves; the distant prospect on the land side, islanded with sunshine; the sea, like a basin full to the margin; the dark fresh-ploughed fields; the turnips of a lively rough green. Returned through the wood.

February 25th. I lay down in the morning, though the whole day was very pleasant, and the evening fine. We did not walk.

February 26th. Coleridge came in the morning, and Mr. and Mrs. Cruikshank; walked with Coleridge nearly to Stowey after dinner. A very clear afternoon. We lay sidelong upon the turf, and gazed on the landscape till it melted into more than natural loveliness. The sea very uniform, of a pale greyish blue, only one distant bay, bright and blue as a sky; had there been a vessel sailing up it, a perfect image of delight. Walked to the top of a high hill to see a fortification. Again sat down to feed upon the prospect; a magnificent scene, *curiously* spread out for even minute inspection, though so extensive that the mind is afraid to calculate its bounds. A winter prospect shows every cottage, every farm, and the forms of distant trees, such as in summer have no distinguishing mark. On our return, Jupiter and Venus before us. While the twilight still overpowered the light of the moon, we were reminded that she was shining bright above our heads, by our faint shadows going before us. We had seen her on the tops of the hills, melting into the blue sky. Poole called while we were absent.

February 27th. I walked to Stowey in the evening. Wm. and Basil went with me through the wood. The prospect bright, yet *mildly* beautiful. The sea big and white, swelled to the very shores, but round and high in the middle. Coleridge returned with me, as far as the wood. A very bright moonlight night. Venus almost like another moon. Lost to us at Alfoxden long before she goes down the large white sea.

. . . . .

THE COTTAGER TO HER INFANT

The days are cold, the nights are long,
The north-wind sings a doleful song;
Then hush again upon my breast;
All merry things are now at rest,
    Save thee, my pretty Love!

The kitten sleeps upon the hearth,
The crickets long have ceased their mirth;
There's nothing stirring in the house
Save one *wee,* hungry, nibbling mouse,
    Then why so busy thou?

Nay! start not at that sparkling light;
'Tis but the moon that shines so bright
On the window pane bedropped with rain:
Then, little Darling! sleep again,
    And wake when it is day.

COMPOSED IN 1805 BY
DOROTHY WORDSWORTH

William Wordsworth
Some Selected Poems

A NIGHT-PIECE

———— The sky is overcast
With a continuous cloud of texture close,
Heavy and wan, all whitened by the Moon,
Which through that veil is indistinctly seen,
A dull, contracted circle, yielding light
So feebly spread that not a shadow falls,
Chequering the ground—from rock, plant, tree, or tower.
At length a pleasant instantaneous gleam
Startles the pensive traveller while he treads
His lonesome path, with unobserving eye
Bent earthwards; he looks up—the clouds are split
Asunder,—and above his head he sees
The clear Moon, and the glory of the heavens.
There, in a black-blue vault she sails along,
Followed by multitudes of stars, that, small
And sharp, and bright, along the dark abyss
Drive as she drives: how fast they wheel away,
Yet vanish not!—the wind is in the tree,
But they are silent;—still they roll along
Immeasurably distant; and the vault,
Built round by those white clouds,
   enormous clouds,
Still deepens its unfathomable depth.
At length the Vision closes; and the mind,
Not undisturbed by the delight it feels,
Which slowly settles into peaceful calm,
Is left to muse upon the solemn scene.

COMPOSED IN 1798

211

THERE WAS A BOY

There was a Boy; ye knew him well, ye cliffs
And islands of Winander!—many a time,
At evening, when the earliest stars began
To move along the edges of the hills,
Rising or setting, would he stand alone,
Beneath the trees, or by the glimmering lake;
And there, with fingers interwoven, both hands
Pressed closely palm to palm and to his mouth
Uplifted, he, as through an instrument,
Blew mimic hootings to the silent owls,
That they might answer him.—And they would shout
Across the watery vale, and shout again,
Responsive to his call,—with quivering peals,
And long halloos, and screams, and echoes loud
Redoubled and redoubled; concourse wild
Of jocund din! And, when there came a pause
Of silence such as baffled his best skill:
Then, sometimes, in that silence, while he hung
Listening, a gentle shock of mild surprise
Has carried far into his heart the voice
Of mountain-torrents; or the visible scene
Would enter unawares into his mind
With all its solemn imagery, its rocks,
Its woods, and that uncertain heaven received
Into the bosom of the steady lake.
    This boy was taken from his mates, and died
In childhood, ere he was full twelve years old.
Pre-eminent in beauty is the vale
Where he was born and bred: the church-yard hangs
Upon a slope above the village-school;
And, through that churchyard when my way has led
On summer-evenings, I believe, that there

A long half-hour together I have stood
Mute—looking at the grave in which he lies!

TO MY SISTER

It is the first mild day of March:
Each minute sweeter than before,
The redbreast sings from the tall larch
That stands beside our door.

There is a blessing in the air,
Which seems a sense of joy to yield
To the bare trees, and mountains bare,
And grass in the green field.

My sister! ('tis a wish of mine)
Now that our morning meal is done,
Make haste, your morning task resign;
Come forth and feel the sun.

Edward will come with you;—and, pray,
Put on with speed your woodland dress;
And bring no book: for this one day
We'll give to idleness.

No joyless forms shall regulate
Our living calendar:
We from to-day, my Friend, will date
The opening of the year.

Love, now a universal birth,
From heart to heart is stealing,
From earth to man, from man to earth:
—It is the hour of feeling.

One moment now may give us more
Than years of toiling reason:

Our minds shall drink at every pore
The spirit of the season.

Some silent laws our hearts will make,
Which they shall long obey:
We for the year to come may take
Our temper from to-day.

And from the blessed power that rolls
About, below, above,
We'll frame the measure of our souls:
They shall be tuned to love.

Then come, my Sister! come, I pray,
With speed put on your woodland dress;
And bring no book: for this one day
We'll give to idleness.

COMPOSED IN 1798

WE ARE SEVEN

—A simple Child,
That lightly draws its breath,
And feels its life in every limb,
What should it know of death?

I met a little cottage Girl:
She was eight years old, she said;
Her hair was thick with many a curl
That clustered round her head.

She had a rustic, woodland air,
And she was wildly clad:
Her eyes were fair, and very fair;
—Her beauty made me glad.

"Sisters and brothers, little Maid,
How many may you be?"

214

"How many? Seven in all," she said,
And wondering looked at me.

"And where are they? I pray you tell."
She answered, "Seven are we;
And two of us at Conway dwell,
And two are gone to sea.

"Two of us in the church-yard lie,
My sister and my brother;
And, in the church-yard cottage, I
Dwell near them with my mother."

"You say that two at Conway dwell,
And two are gone to sea,
Yet ye are seven!—I pray you tell,
Sweet Maid, how this may be."

Then did the little Maid reply,
"Seven boys and girls are we;
Two of us in the church-yard lie,
Beneath the church-yard tree."

"You run about, my little Maid,
Your limbs they are alive;
If two are in the church-yard laid,
Then ye are only five."

"Their graves are green, they may be seen,"
The little Maid replied,
"Twelve steps or more from my mother's door,
And they are side by side.

"My stockings there I often knit,
My kerchief there I hem;
And there upon the ground I sit,
And sing a song to them.

"And often after sun-set, Sir,
When it is light and fair,

I take my little porringer,
And eat my supper there.

"The first that died was sister Jane;
In bed she moaning lay,
Till God released her of her pain;
And then she went away.

"So in the church-yard she was laid;
And, when the grass was dry,
Together round her grave we played,
My brother John and I.

"And when the ground was white with snow,
And I could run and slide,
My brother John was forced to go,
And he lies by her side."

"How many are you, then," said I,
"If they two are in heaven?"
Quick was the little Maid's reply,
"O Master! we are seven."

"But they are dead; those two are dead!
Their spirits are in heaven!"
'Twas throwing words away; for still
The little Maid would have her will,
And said, "Nay, we are seven!"

COMPOSED IN 1798

"SHE DWELT AMONG THE UNTRODDEN WAYS"

She dwelt among the untrodden ways
    Beside the springs of Dove,
A Maid whom there were none to praise
    And very few to love:

A violet by a mossy stone
   Half hidden from the eye!
—Fair as a star, when only one
   Is shining in the sky.

She lived unknown, and few could know
   When Lucy ceased to be;
But she is in her grave, and, oh,
   The difference to me!

COMPOSED IN 1799

TO M. H.

Our walk was far among the ancient trees:
There was no road, nor any woodman's path;
But a thick umbrage—checking the wild growth
Of weed and sapling, along soft green turf
Beneath the branches—of itself had made
A track, that brought us to a slip of lawn,
And a small bed of water in the woods.
All round this pool both flocks and herds might drink
On its firm margin, even as from a well,
Or some stone-basin which the herdsman's hand
Had shaped for their refreshment; nor did sun,
Or wind from any quarter, ever come,
But as a blessing to this calm recess,
This glade of water and this one green field.
The spot was made by Nature for herself;
The travellers know it not, and 'twill remain
Unknown to them; but it is beautiful;
And if a man should plant his cottage near,
Should sleep beneath the shelter of its trees,
And blend its waters with his daily meal,

He would so love it, that in his death-hour
Its image would survive among his thoughts:
And therefore, my sweet Mary, this still Nook,
With all its beeches, we have named from You!

COMPOSED IN 1799
To Mary Hutchinson
Whom William Wordsworth
Married

THE SPARROW'S NEST

Behold, within the leafy shade,
Those bright blue eggs together laid!
On me the chance-discovered sight
Gleamed like a vision of delight.
I started—seeming to espy
The home and sheltered bed,
The Sparrow's dwelling, which, hard by
My Father's house, in wet or dry
My sister Emmeline and I
  Together visited.

She looked at it and seemed to fear it;
Dreading, tho' wishing, to be near it:
Such heart was in her, being then
A little Prattler among men.
The Blessing of my later years
Was with me when a boy:
She gave me eyes, she gave me ears;
And humble cares, and delicate fears;
A heart, the fountain of sweet tears;
  And love, and thought, and joy.

COMPOSED IN 1801

"MY HEART LEAPS UP WHEN I BEHOLD"

My heart leaps up when I behold
    A rainbow in the sky:
So was it when my life began;
So is it now I am a man;
So be it when I shall grow old,
    Or let me die!
The Child is father of the Man;
And I could wish my days to be
Bound each to each by natural piety.

COMPOSED IN 1802

"AMONG ALL LOVELY THINGS
MY LOVE HAD BEEN"

Among all lovely things my Love had been;
Had noted well the stars, all flowers that grew
About her home; but she had never seen
A glow-worm, never one, and this I knew.

While riding near her home one stormy night
A single glow-worm did I chance to espy;
I gave a fervent welcome to the sight,
And from my Horse I leapt; great joy had I.

Upon a leaf the glow-worm did I lay,
To bear it with me through the stormy night:
And, as before, it shone without dismay;
Albeit putting forth a fainter light.

When to the dwelling of my Love I came,
I went into the orchard quietly;

219

And left the glow-worm, blessing it by name,
Laid safely by itself, beneath a tree.

The whole next day, I hoped, and hoped with fear;
At night the glow-worm shone beneath the tree:
I led my Lucy to the spot, "Look here,"
Oh! joy it was for her, and joy for me!

COMPOSED IN 1802

WRITTEN IN MARCH

While resting on the bridge at the foot of Brother's Water

The Cock is crowing,
The stream is flowing,
The small birds twitter,
The lake doth glitter,
The green field sleeps in the sun;
The oldest and youngest
Are at work with the strongest;
The cattle are grazing,
Their heads never raising;
There are forty feeding like one!

Like an army defeated
The snow hath retreated,
And now doth fare ill
On the top of the bare hill;
The ploughboy is whooping—anon—anon:
There's joy in the mountains;
There's life in the fountains;
Small clouds are sailing,
Blue sky prevailing;
The rain is over and gone!

COMPOSED IN 1802

TO A BUTTERFLY

I've watched you now a full half-hour,
Self-poised upon that yellow flower;
And, little Butterfly! indeed
I know not if you sleep or feed.
How motionless!—not frozen seas
More motionless! and then
What joy awaits you, when the breeze
Hath found you out among the trees,
And calls you forth again!

This plot of orchard-ground is ours;
My trees they are, my Sister's flowers;
Here rest your wings when they are weary;
Here lodge as in a sanctuary!
Come often to us, fear no wrong;
Sit near us on the bough!
We'll talk of sunshine and of song,
And summer days, when we were young;
Sweet childish days, that were as long
As twenty days are now.

COMPOSED IN 1802

TO A SKY-LARK

Up with me! up with me into the clouds!
    For thy song, Lark, is strong;
Up with me, up with me into the clouds!
    Singing, singing,
With clouds and sky about thee ringing,
    Lift me, guide me till I find
That spot which seems so to thy mind!

I have walked through wildernesses dreary,
And to-day my heart is weary;
Had I now the wings of a Faery,
Up to thee would I fly.
There is madness about thee, and joy divine
In that song of thine;
Lift me, guide me high and high
To thy banqueting-place in the sky.

Joyous as morning,
Thou art laughing and scorning;
Thou hast a nest for thy love and thy rest,
And, though little troubled with sloth,
Drunken Lark! thous wouldst be loth
To be such a traveller as I.
Happy, happy Liver,
With a soul as strong as a mountain river
Pouring out praise to the almighty Giver,
Joy and jollity be with us both!

Alas! my journey, rugged and uneven,
Through prickly moors or dusty ways must wind;
But hearing thee, or others of thy kind,
As full of gladness and as free of heaven,
I, with my fate contented, will plod on,
And hope for higher raptures, when life's day is done.

COMPOSED IN 1805

"IT IS A BEAUTEOUS EVENING, CALM AND FREE"

It is a beauteous evening, calm and free,
The holy time is quiet as a Nun
Breathless with adoration; the broad sun
Is sinking down in its tranquillity;

The gentleness of heaven broods o'er the Sea:
Listen! the mighty Being is awake,
And doth with his eternal motion make
A sound like thunder—everlastingly.
Dear Child! dear Girl! that walkest with me here,
If thou appear untouched by solemn thought,
Thy nature is not therefore less divine:
Thou liest in Abraham's bosom all the year;
And worship'st at the Temple's inner shrine,
God being with thee when we know it not.

COMPOSED IN 1802

"I WANDERED LONELY AS A CLOUD"

I wandered lonely as a cloud
That floats on high o'er vales and hills,
When all at once I saw a crowd,
A host, of golden daffodils;
Beside the lake, beneath the trees,
Fluttering and dancing in the breeze.

Continuous as the stars that shine
And twinkle on the milky way,
They stretched in never-ending line
Along the margin of a bay:
Ten thousand saw I at a glance,
Tossing their heads in sprightly dance.

The waves beside them danced; but they
Out-did the sparkling waves in glee:
A poet could not but be gay,
In such a jocund company:
I gazed—and gazed—but little thought
What wealth the show to me had brought:

For oft, when on my couch I lie
In vacant or in pensive mood,
They flash upon that inward eye
Which is the bliss of solitude;
And then my heart with pleasure fills,
And dances with the daffodils.

COMPOSED IN 1804

"SHE WAS A PHANTOM OF DELIGHT"

She was a Phantom of delight
When first she gleamed upon my sight;
A lovely Apparition, sent
To be a moment's ornament;
Her eyes as stars of Twilight fair;
Like Twilight's, too, her dusky hair;
But all things else about her drawn
From May-time and the cheerful Dawn;
A dancing Shape, an Image gay,
To haunt, to startle, and way-lay.

I saw her upon nearer view,
A Spirit, yet a Woman too!
Her household motions light and free,
And steps of virgin-liberty;
A countenance in which did meet
Sweet records, promises as sweet;
A Creature not too bright or good
For human nature's daily food;
For transient sorrows, simple wiles,
Praise, blame, love, kisses, tears, and smiles.

And now I see with eye serene
The very pulse of the machine;
A Being breathing thoughtful breath,

A Traveller between life and death;
The reason firm, the temperate will,
Endurance, foresight, strength, and skill;
A perfect Woman, nobly planned,
To warn, to comfort, and command;
And yet a Spirit still, and bright
With something of angelic light.

COMPOSED IN 1804

THE SOLITARY REAPER

Behold her, single in the field,
Yon solitary Highland Lass!
Reaping and singing by herself;
Stop here, or gently pass!
Alone she cuts and binds the grain,
And sings a melancholy strain;
O listen! for the Vale profound
Is overflowing with the sound.

No Nightingale did ever chaunt
More welcome notes to weary bands
Of travellers in some shady haunt,
Among Arabian sands:
A voice so thrilling ne'er was heard
In spring-time from the Cuckoo-bird,
Breaking the silence of the seas
Among the farthest Hebrides.

Will no one tell me what she sings?—
Perhaps the plaintive numbers flow
For old, unhappy, far-off things,
And battles long ago:
Or is it some more humble lay,

Familiar matter of to-day?
Some natural sorrow, loss, or pain,
That has been, and may be again?

Whate'er the theme, the Maiden sang
As if her song could have no ending;
I saw her singing at her work,
And o'er the sickle bending;—
I listened, motionless and still;
And, as I mounted up the hill,
The music in my heart I bore,
Long after it was heard no more.

COMPOSED IN 1805

"THE WORLD IS TOO MUCH WITH US;
LATE AND SOON"

The world is too much with us; late and soon,
Getting and spending, we lay waste our powers:
Little we see in Nature that is ours;
We have given our hearts away, a sordid boon!
This Sea that bares her bosom to the moon;
The winds that will be howling at all hours,
And are up-gathered now like sleeping flowers;
For this, for everything, we are out of tune;
It moves us not.—Great God! I'd rather be
A Pagan suckled in a creed outworn;
So might I, standing on this pleasant lea,
Have glimpses that would make me less forlorn;
Have sight of Proteus rising from the sea;
Or hear old Triton blow his wreathèd horn.

COMPOSED IN 1806

GIPSIES

Yet are they here the same unbroken knot
Of human Beings, in the self-same spot!
    Men, women, children, yea the frame
    Of the whole spectacle the same!
Only their fire seems bolder, yielding light,
Now deep and red, the colouring of night;
    That on their Gipsy-faces falls,
    Their bed of straw and blanket-walls.
—Twelve hours, twelve bounteous hours are gone, while I
Have been a traveller under open sky,
    Much witnessing of change and cheer,
    Yet as I left I find them here!
The weary Sun betook himself to rest;—
Then issued Vesper from the fulgent west,
    Outshining like a visible God
    The glorious path in which he trod.
And now, ascending, after one dark hour
And one night's diminution of her power,
    Behold the mighty Moon! this way
    She looks as if at them—but they
Regard not her:—oh better wrong and strife
(By nature transient) than this torpid life;
    Life which the very stars reprove
    As on their silent tasks they move!
Yet, witness all that stirs in heaven or earth!
In scorn I speak not;—they are what their birth
    And breeding suffer them to be;
    Wild outcasts of society!

COMPOSED IN 1807

"I DROPPED MY PEN"

I dropped my pen; and listened to the Wind
That sang of trees uptorn and vessels tost—

A midnight harmony; and wholly lost
To the general sense of men by chains confined
Of business, care, or pleasure; or resigned
To timely sleep. Thought I, the impassioned strain,
Which, without aid of numbers, I sustain,
Like acceptation from the World will find.
Yet some with apprehensive ear shall drink
A dirge devoutly breathed o'er sorrows past;
And to the attendant promise will give heed—
The prophecy,—like that of this wild blast,
Which, while it makes the heart with sadness shrink,
Tells also of bright calms that shall succeed.

COMPOSED IN 1808

"SURPRISED BY JOY—
IMPATIENT AS THE WIND"

Surprised by joy—impatient as the Wind
I turned to share the transport—Oh! with whom
But Thee, deep buried in the silent tomb,
That spot which no vicissitude can find?
Love, faithful love, recalled thee to my mind—
But how could I forget thee? Through what power,
Even for the least division of an hour,
Have I been so beguiled as to be blind
To my most grievous loss!—That thought's return
Was the worst pang that sorrow ever bore,
Save one, one only, when I stood forlorn,
Knowing my heart's best treasure was no more;
That neither present time, nor years unborn
Could to my sight that heavenly face restore.

COMPOSED LATER THAN JUNE, 1812
BUT PRINTED IN 1815

AIREY-FORCE VALLEY

————Not a breath of air
Ruffles the bosom of this leafy glen.
From the brook's margin, wide around, the trees
Are stedfast as the rocks; the brook itself,
Old as the hills that feed it from afar,
Doth rather deepen than disturb the calm
Where all things else are still and motionless.
And yet, even now, a little breeze, perchance
Escaped from boisterous winds that rage without,
Has entered, by the sturdy oaks unfelt,
But to its gentle touch how sensitive
Is the light ash! that, pendent from the brow
Of yon dim cave, in seeming silence makes
A soft eye-music of slow-waving boughs,
Powerful almost as vocal harmony
To stay the wanderer's steps and soothe his thoughts.

COMPOSED IN 1836

ULLSWATER, FROM NEAR GOWBARROW
The spot where bloomed "a host of golden daffodils"

Important Dates
in the Lives of Dorothy and William Wordsworth

1770   William Wordsworth was born at Cockermouth in England on April 7.

1771   Dorothy Wordsworth was born in the same village on Christmas Day.

1778   Ann Cookson Wordsworth, Dorothy and William's mother, died.

1779   William was sent to school at Hawkshead; Dorothy was sent to live with her mother's cousin, Miss Elizabeth Threlkeld.

1783   John Wordsworth, Dorothy and William's father, died.

1787   William went to St. John's College, Cambridge. Dorothy went to live with her Uncle William Cookson and his new bride, Dorothy Cowper, in Forncett in Norfolk.

1789   The French Revolution exploded.

1790   William and his friend Robert Jones undertook a walking tour in France, Switzerland, and Italy. William returned to England.

1791   William returned to France.

1792   William met and fell in love with Annette Vallon.

William met many revolutionary republicans and made a special friend of Michel Beaupuy.

He returned to England in December, the same month that his daughter Caroline was born in France.

1793 War between France and England.

1794 Dorothy was reunited with William. Her family accused her "of rambling about the country on foot." She became for the first time her brother's secretary and copyist.

1795 Raisley Calvert bequeathed a legacy of £900 to William. Dorothy and William moved to Racedown Lodge in Dorset.

1796 William wrote *The Borderers,* a tragedy in blank verse. William met Samuel Taylor Coleridge in Bristol.

1797 William wrote *The Ruined Cottage* about an old pedlar. Parts of it were to be incorporated into *The Prelude.* The concept of the Pedlar was turned into the Wanderer of *The Excursion.*

Coleridge visited Racedown. He, William, and Dorothy went to Nether Stowey in Somerset. In July, William and Dorothy rented Alfoxden House in the Quantocks.

William began to work on the poems to be published as *Lyrical Ballads.*

Coleridge wrote *Kubla Khan* and began *The Ancient Mariner.*

1798 Dorothy began her journal.

Coleridge completed *The Ancient Mariner* and the first part of *Christabel.*

William began *The Prelude* and wrote *Tintern Abbey.*

The three friends were inseparable. "We are," said Coleridge, "three people, but one soul."

Lyrical Ballads was published.

In September, Dorothy, William, and Coleridge went to Germany.

1799 Dorothy and William lived in Goslar in Germany.

They returned to England where they spent time with the Hutchinsons.

William became deeply interested in Mary Hutchinson.

Dorothy and William moved into Dove Cottage, in Town End, Grasmere.

1800 Coleridge moved into Greta Hall, Keswick.

John Wordsworth visited at Dove Cottage.

William worked on poems for a new edition of *Lyrical Ballads,* published in two volumes.

1801 Mary Hutchinson made a long visit to Dove Cottage.

1802 A year, for William, of great poetical activity. Among other poems, he started the *Ode: Intimations of Immortality.*

Dorothy and William received a legacy from their father. The money allowed him to marry Mary Hutchinson in October after a trip with Dorothy to see Annette in France.

1803 Mary and William became parents for the first time with the birth of John.

Coleridge's brother-in-law, Robert Southey and his family, move into Greta Hall.

Dorothy, William, and Samuel made a trip to Scotland.

1804 Dorothy, called Dora, was born to Mary and William. She was named Dorothy, explained William, because the name "had so long been devoted in my own thoughts to the first daughter that I might have that I could not break my promise to myself—a promise in which my wife participated." The name Dorothy, however, had become "old fashioned," and the girl was always referred to as Dora.

Coleridge's health deteriorated and he sailed for Malta.

1805 The "set is broken" when John Wordsworth drowned.

The Prelude is finished but not published until William's death.

1806 Thomas Wordsworth was born.

Coleridge and the Wordsworths spend the winter in Coleorton at Sir George Beaumont's estate.

1807 Thomas De Quincey visited the Wordsworths.

1808 Catherine Wordsworth was born.
      The Wordsworths moved to a larger home, Allan Bank.

1810 William Wordsworth was born.
      The friendship with Coleridge was deteriorating and a violent quarrel resulted.

1811 The peripatetic Wordsworths moved again, this time to Grasmere Vicarage.

1812 Catherine and Thomas Wordsworth died. The entire family suffered a depression.

1813 William became Distributor of Stamps for Westmoreland, a governmental sinecure.
      The family moved to Rydal Mount.

1814 *The Excursion* was published and William bitterly attacked.

1815 *Miscellaneous Poems* published. The Battle of Waterloo. Wordsworth grew far more conservative in politics.

1816 Caroline, William's daughter, was married in France.

1817 William became an important literary figure in London where he met many of the younger generation of poets including John Keats.

1818–1832 Wordsworth reworked many poems and traveled as often as possible.

1834 Samuel Taylor Coleridge's death.
      Death of Charles Lamb.

1835 Dorothy Wordsworth had a breakdown from which she never recovered.

1837 Queen Victoria came to the throne and a new age began.

1841 Dora married Edward Quillinan.

1843 William Wordsworth became Poet Laureate.

1847 Dora Quillinan, after years of fragile health, died.

1850 William Wordsworth died on April 23.
      The Prelude was published; the title was given by Mary Wordsworth.

1855 The death of Dorothy Wordsworth.

Bibliography

Allott, Kenneth (ed.) *The Pelican Book of English Prose, Vol. 3, Eighteenth Century Prose 1700–1780* (D. W. Jefferson, ed.). Baltimore, Maryland: Penguin Books, Inc., 1956.

Bagley, Arthur L., *Holiday Rambles in the English Lake District*. London: Skeffington & Son, Ltd., n.d.

Batho, Edith C., *The Later Wordsworth*. New York: Russell & Russell, Inc., 1963.

Bayne-Powell, Rosamond, *The English Child in the Eighteenth Century*. New York: E. P. Dutton & Co., Inc., 1939.

Beatty, Arthur, *William Wordsworth: His Doctrine and Art in Their Historical Relations*. Madison: The University of Wisconsin Press, 1962.

Beatty, Frederika, *William Wordsworth of Dove Cottage*. New York: Bookman Associates, Inc., 1964.

Besant, Walter, *Fifty Years Ago*. New York: Harper & Brothers, 1888.

Blanshard, Frances, *Portraits of Wordsworth*. London: George Allen and Unwin, Ltd., 1959.

Blunden, Edmund, *Charles Lamb and His Contemporaries*. Hamden, Connecticut: Archon Books, 1967.

Bradley, A. G., *Highways and Byways in the Lake District*. London: Macmillan and Co., Ltd., 1919.

Caine, T. Hall, *Cobwebs of Criticism*. London: Elliot Stock, 62, Paternoster Row, E. G., 1883.

Carpenter, Maurice, *The Indifferent Horseman: The Divine Comedy of Samuel Taylor Coleridge*. London: Elek Books, 1954.

Bibliography

Clive, John, *Scotch Reviewers: The Edinburgh Review, 1802–1875.* Cambridge, Massachusetts: Harvard University Press, 1957.

Coburn, Kathleen (ed.), *Inquiring Spirit: A Coleridge Reader.* New York: Minerva Press, 1951.

Coe, Charles Norton, *Wordsworth and the Literature of Travel.* New York: Bookman Associates, 1953.

Coleridge, Samuel Taylor, *Selected Poetry and Prose* (ed. Stephen Potter). London: The Nonesuch Press, 1933.

Coleridge, Samuel Taylor, *Biographia Literaria or Biographical Sketches of My Literary Life and Opinions* (2 Vols.). London: William Pickering, 1847.

Coleridge, Sara, *Memoir and Letters.* New York: Harper & Brothers.

Country Life, *Picture Book of the Lake District.* London: Country Life Limited, 1961.

Darbishire, Helen (ed.), *Journal of Dorothy Wordsworth.* London: Oxford University Press, 1958.

De Quincey, Thomas, *Autobiographic Sketches.* New York: Hurd and Houghton, 1876.

De Quincey, Thomas, *Biographical Essays.* Boston: Ticknor, Reed and Fields, 1850.

De Quincey, Thomas, *Literary Reminiscences* (2 Vols.). Boston: Ticknor, Reed and Fields, 1851.

De Quincey, Thomas, *Miscellaneous Essays.* Boston: Ticknor, Reed and Fields, 1851.

De Quincey, Thomas, *Selected Writings* (see Philip Van Doren Stern, ed.). New York: Random House, 1937.

de Selincourt, Ernest, *Dorothy Wordsworth, a Biography.* Oxford: The Clarendon Press, 1965.

Douglas, Wallace W., *The Construction of a Personality.* Kent State University Press, 1968.

Eliot, T. S., *On Poetry and Poets.* New York: The Noonday Press, 1968.

Ellis, Amanda M., *Rebels and Conservatives: Dorothy and William Wordsworth and Their Circle.* Bloomington, Indiana: Indiana University Press, 1967.

Fink, Z. S. (ed.), *The Early Wordsworthian Milieu.* Oxford: The Clarendon Press, 1958.

Ford, Boris (ed.), *Pelican Guide to English Literature from Blake to Byron.* Baltimore: Penguin Books, 1961.

Bibliography

Fussell, G. E. & K. R., *The English Countrywoman*. London: Andrew Melrose, 1953.

George, Dorothy M., *England in Transition*. London: Penguin Books, 1953.

Goodwin, Michael (ed.), *Nineteenth-Century Opinion*. Harmondsworth-Middlesex, Great Britain: Penguin Books, Ltd., 1951.

Grant, Michael, *Cambridge*. London: Reynal & Co. in association with William Morrow & Co., 1966.

Halliday, F. E., *Wordsworth and His World*. New York: The Viking Press, 1970.

Havens, Raymond Dexter, *The Mind of a Poet* (2 Vols.). Baltimore: The Johns Hopkins Press, 1941.

Hazlitt, W. Carew (Col.), *Mary and Charles Lamb: Poems, Letters and Remains*. London: Chatto and Windus, 1874.

Healey, George Harris (compiler), *The Cornell Wordsworth Collection*. Ithaca, New York: Cornell University Press, 1957.

Herford, C. H., *The Age of Wordsworth*. London: G. Bell and Sons, Ltd., 1911.

Hill, Julian, *Great English Poets*. London: E. Grant Richards, 1907.

Hoys, Dudley, *English Lake Country*. London: B. T. Batsford Ltd., 1969.

Hunt, William, *Historic Towns, Bristol*. London: Longmans, Green & Co., 1889.

Hutchinson, Sara, *Letters from 1800 to 1835* (ed. Kathleen Coburn). Toronto: University of Toronto Press, 1954.

Jeffrey, Francis, *Essays on English Poets and Poetry from the Edinburgh Review* (1808–25). London: George Routledge & Sons, Ltd.

Johnson, E. D. H., *The Poetry of Earth*. New York: Atheneum, 1966.

Jordan, John E., *De Quincey to Wordsworth, a Biography of a Relationship*. Berkeley, Los Angeles: University of California Press, 1962.

Lamb, Charles, *Letters*, 2 Vols. (ed. Alfred Ainger). London: Macmillan & Co., Ltd., 1904.

Lamb, Charles, *Life, Letters, Writings*, 6 Vols. (ed. Percy Fitzgerald). London: John Slark, 1882.

Lamb, Mary and Charles, *Poem, Letters and Remains* (see W. Carew Hazlitt). London: Chatto and Windus, 1874.

Lee, Edmund, *Dorothy Wordsworth: The Story of a Sister's Love*. London: Dames Clarke & Co., 1894.

Legouis, Emile, *William Wordsworth and Annette Vallon*. Hamden, Connecticut: Archon Books, 1967.

Lindenberger, Herbert, *On Wordsworth's Prelude*. Princeton, New Jersey: Princeton University Press, 1963.

Lowes, John L., *The Road to Xanadu: A Study in the Ways of the Imagination*. Boston and New York: Houghton Mifflin Co., 1927.

Matthews, T. S. (ed.), *The Selected Letters of Charles Lamb*. New York: Farrar, Straus and Cudahy, 1956.

Moorman, Mary, *William Wordsworth, A Biography*. Oxford: The Clarendon Press, 1957.

Moorman, Mary, *William Wordsworth, A Biography: The Later Years 1803–1850*. Oxford: The Clarendon Press, 1965.

Oliphant, Mrs., *The Literary History of England* (3 Vols.). London: Macmillan & Co., 1889.

Quiller-Couch, Sir Arthur (ed.), *The Oxford Book of English Verse*. Oxford: The Clarendon Press, 1939.

Read, Herbert, *The True Voice of Feeling: Studies in English Romantic Poetry*. New York: Pantheon Books, Inc., 1953.

Read, Herbert, *Wordsworth*. New York: Jonathan Cape and Harrison Smith, 1931.

Reed, Mark L., *Wordsworth, the Chronology of the Early Years, 1770–1799*. Cambridge, Mass.: Harvard University Press, 1967.

Richards, I. A., *Coleridge on Imagination*. London: Kegan Paul, Trench, Trubner & Co., Ltd., 1934.

Rugg, Harold, *Imagination*. New York: Harper & Row, 1963.

Salvesen, Christopher, *The Landscape of Memory: A Study of Wordsworth's Poetry*. Lincoln, Nebraska: University of Nebraska Press, 1965.

Schneider, Ben Ross, Jr., *Wordsworth's Cambridge Education*. Cambridge, England: The University Press, 1957.

Stephen, Leslie, *Samuel Johnson*. New York: Harper & Brother, 1879.

Stern, Philip Van Doren, *Selected Writings of Thomas De Quincey*. New York: Random House, 1937.

Sydenham, M. J., *The French Revolution*. New York: Capricorn Books, 1966.

Talfourd, Thomas Noon, *The Life and Letters of Charles Lamb*. New York: H. W. Derby, 1861.

Thompson, J. M., *Robespierre and the French Revolution*. New York: Collier Books, 1967.

Williams, Charles, *Reason and Beauty in the Poetic Mind*. Oxford: The Clarendon Press, 1933.

Bibliography

Wordsworth, Christopher, *Memoirs of William Wordsworth, Poet-Laureate, D.C.L.* (2 Vols.). Boston: Ticknor, Reed & Fields, 1851.

Wordsworth, Dorothy, *The Alfoxden Journal, 1798. The Grasmere Journals, 1800–1803.* (See Darbishire (ed.) Journals of Dorothy Wordsworth). London: Oxford Unversity Press, 1958.

Wordsworth, Dorothy, *Recollections of a Tour Made in Scotland, A.D. 1803.* Edinburgh: Edmonston and Douglas, 1874.

Wordsworth, Mary, *Letters, 1800–1855* (ed. Mary E. Burton). Oxford: The Clarendon Press, 1958.

Wordsworth, William and Dorothy, *Letters, The Early Years, 1787–1805* (ed. Ernest de Selincourt, rev. Chester L. Shaver). Oxford: The Clarendon Press, 1967.

Wordsworth, William, *Poetical Works* (ed. Thomas Hutchinson, rev. Ernest de Selincourt). London: Oxford University Press, 1965.

Wordsworth, William, *Poetical Works, 5. Vols.* (ed. E. de Selincourt and Helen Darbishire). Oxford: The Clarendon Press, 1966.

Wordsworth, William, *The Prelude or Growth of a Poet's Mind* (ed. Ernest de Selincourt, rev. Helen Darbishire). Oxford: The Clarendon Press. 1959.

Wordsworth, William, *Poetical Works.* (int. by W. M. Rossetti.) London: E. Moxon, Son & Co., n.d.

Woodring, Carl, *Wordsworth.* Boston: Houghton Mifflin Company, 1965.

Acknowledgments

I am deeply appreciative to my friends in and around the Lake
Country in England whose contemporary affection for the Wordsworths and their friends gave the writing of this book a particular
immediacy. I can remember my very first visit to Dove Cottage
when one of the curators, a true gentlewoman who might have
stepped out of the eighteenth century, invited my family into
her world—a world in which Dorothy was still so alive that she
was probably in the garden with the columbines, while Willie
was just beyond at his favorite cataract, and the table was obviously set for Coleridge who momentarily might arrive for tea.
The "creative presence" of this circle of friends still lingers in this
last quarter of the twentieth century and their love of nature and
of "place" seems more pertinent than ever.

For specific help in the preparation of this book I am grateful
to Mrs. Orma Collin, who checked all details about the countryside in which she grew up; to Mrs. Clara Pye; to the staff of Vanguard Press; to the designer of the book, Ernst Reichl; and to his
daughter, Ruth Reichl, whose jacket so caught the spirit of a
landscape that I love.

Once again I am indebted to Susan Belcher, who not only lent
me her wits and her patience, but even her family's waterfall and
pond, a Wordsworthian setting, that added another "presence"
to this book.

I must also thank the staff of the Cornell Wordsworth Collection of Cornell University, the Greenwich (Connecticut) Book
Shop, Meads of Greenwich, the Greenwich Library, and the many
antiquarian bookshops that hunted down material I needed.

Finally, a special appreciation to all those who planted daffodils.